Willie Silleck

Reliable cook book

Willie Silleck

Reliable cook book

ISBN/EAN: 9783744785952

Printed in Europe, USA, Canada, Australia, Japan

Cover: Foto ©Lupo / pixelio.de

More available books at **www.hansebooks.com**

RELIABLE
COOK BOOK,

COMPILED BY

MISS WILLIE SILLECK,

IN AID OF

Industrial School and Home for Destitute Children.

"We may live without poetry, music and art;
We may live without conscience, and live without heart;
We may live without friends, we may live without books;
But civilized man cannot live without cooks.
He may live without books—what is knowledge but grieving?
He may live without hope—what is hope but deceiving?
He may live without love—what is passion but pining?
But where is the man that can live without dining?"

LUCILE.

NEW YORK:
D. H. GILDERSLEEVE & CO., PRINTERS, 101 CHAMBERS STREET.

1878.

INDUSTRIAL SCHOOL AND HOME FOR DESTITUTE CHILDREN,

BUTLER ST., near VANDERBILT AVE.,

BROOKLYN, N. Y.

PREFACE.

A double interest manifests itself in offering this work to the generous public. First, the proceeds will aid in promoting the welfare of a most praiseworthy charitable institution, known as the "Industrial School Association and Home for Destitute Children of Brooklyn."

Secondly, as "willful waste makes woful want," and every housekeeper is on the alert for *tried* recipes, these, through the kindness of many Brooklyn ladies, have been furnished. Feeling assured that in this case "too many cooks *will not* spoil the broth," we submit the work to the hearty approbation of all.

CONTENTS.

SOUPS.
Stock for Soup—Stock for Soup No. 2—Corn—Wine—Potato—Okra Gumbo—French—Tomato—Tomato No. 2—Mullagatawny—Cream of Spinach—Scotch Broth—Crab—Cheap Green Pea—Black Bean—Strengthening Broth—Oyster—White—Chicken—Beef—Vermicelli—Soup à la Julienne—Calves' Head—Mock Bisquit... 1-7

FISH, OYSTERS, CLAMS, ETC.
Baked Shad—Lobster Salad—Pickled Shad—Scallops—Scalloped Lobster or Salmon—Lobster Croquettes—Turbot à la Crème—Fish Cakes—Roast Clams—Scalloped Oysters—Fried Oysters—Oysters Baked in Shells—Hard-Shell Crabs—Soft-Shell Crabs—Scalloped Clams—Stewed Eels—Jellied Eels—Pickled Clams—Frying Fish—To Broil Mackerel—Oyster Pie—Fish Chowder—Boiled Salmon—Fried Smelts—Steamed Oysters—Pickled Oysters—Clam Fritters—Potted Shad—Cream Fish—Stewed Terrapin—Clam Chowder... 8-16

MEATS.
Fillet of Veal—Sweetbreads—Roast Beef—Roast Lamb or Mutton—Stuffed Lamb—To Corn Beef—Corned Mutton—Sugar Cured Hams—Ham, *Hartford Club Style*—Baked Ham—Spiced Beef—Pressed Tongue and Ham—Dish for Tea—Stewed Beef—Force Meat Balls—Kidney Omelette—Venison Steaks—To Make Croquette—Beef's Heart—To Boil Corned Beef—Meat Loaf—An Excellent Stew—Baked Calves' Liver—Veal Paté—Nice way to use Cold Meat-Ham and Chicken Pie—Lamb Stew—Collared Pork—Calves' Head Pie—Ropa Alieja—Roast Sweetbreads—Larded Sweetbreads—Beefsteak—Veal Olives—Curing Beef—Beef à la Mode—Yorkshire Pudding—To Dress a Pig's Head—Curried Dishes—French Cutlets—Stewed Tripe—To Bake a Pig—Beef à la Royal—Ham Sandwiches... 17-28

POULTRY, GAME, ETC.
Boned or Pressed Turkey—Directions for Choosing Fowl—Chicken Salad—Chicken Salad No. 2—Boned Chicken—Chicken Croquettes—Potage à la Reine—Jellied Chicken—Potted Pigeons—Stewed Pigeons—Quail or Squab Pie—Prairie Chicken—Quail—Fried Chicken—A Fricassee of Chicken—Turkey—To Boil a Turkey—Chicken Pot Pie 29-35

SALADS, SAUCES, ETC.

Carrot Sauce—Lettuce Salad—Cold Slaw—Dressing for Chopped White Cabbage—Mint Sauce—Pepper Sauce—Chili Sauce—Hot Slaw—Sauce for Mushroom Pâtes—Mayonnaise Sauce—Egg Sauce for Fish—Chicken Salad Dressing—Oyster Stuffing for Poultry—Essence of Celery—Stuffing for Turkey—Goose Stuffing—Drawn Butter—Potato Salad—Anchovy Sauce—Caper Sauce. 36-41

EGGS.

Omelette—Omelette, No. 2—Omelette Soufflé—Salad Eggs—Baked Omelette—Omelette Soufflé—Poached Eggs—Boiled Eggs—To Test Eggs—To Preserve Eggs.................................. 42-44

VEGETABLES.

White Potatoes—Sweet Potatoes—To Cook Potatoes under Meat—Corn Chowder—Potato Chips—Corn and Tomatoes—Potato Croquettes—Cauliflower—To Cook Egg Plant—Escalloped Tomatoes—Asparagus—Green Peas—Spinach—Onions—Turnips—Macaroni—Saratoga Potatoes—String Beans—Stewed Tomatoes—New England Baked Beans—Mushrooms—Lima Beans—Green Corn—Succotash—Stuffed Tomatoes. 45-50

DRINKS.

Coffee—Tea—Chocolate—Cocoa—Choca...................... 51-52

BREAKFAST AND SIDE DISHES.

Fondee—Rice Waffles—Rice Croquettes—Dainty Side Dish—Corn Oysters—Hominy—Oatmeal—German Toast—Maple Syrup for Hot Cakes—Boiled Rice—Oyster Macaroni................... 53-56

BREAD, ETC.

To prepare Potatoes for making into Bread—Home-made Yeast—Bread—To use Compressed Yeast—Steamed Brown Bread—Graham Bread—Steamed Graham Bread—Boiled Indian Bread—Corn Bread—Corn Bread No. 2—Muffins—Third Bread Muffins—Raised Biscuits—Corn Muffins—Parker House Rolls—Rice Pancakes—Muffins—Breakfast Rolls—Vienna Pocket-books—Corn Balls—Wheat Puffs—Breakfast Cakes—Light Tea Biscuit—Johnny Cake—Crumpets—Soda Biscuit—Soda Biscuit No. 2—Indian Pone—Queen Muffins—Rice Muffins—Pop-Overs—Rice Cakes—Indian Cakes—Rye Pancakes—Rusk—Rye Cakes—Oatmeal Cakes—Graham Puffs—Waffles—Currant Buns—Bran Muffins—French Rolls—Rye Drop Cakes—Puffs—Straws—Squash Biscuit—Buckwheat Cakes—Soft Waffles—Puffet—Farina Griddle Cakes... 57-68

PUDDINGS AND SAUCES.

Suet—Indian—Chocolate—Delmonico—Baked Blackberry—Cottage—Batter—Tapioca—Randall—Back-About—English Plum—Boiled—German Puffs—Graham—Chocolate—Brown Betty—Apple Slump—English Plum—Sponge—Fried Bread—Kiss—Orange—Cracker—Batter—Whitpot—Whortleberry—Boiled Suet—Orange Fritters—Creme Frite—Peach or Apple Fritters—Webster—Cocoanut—Evening Post—Puff—Green Corn—Apple or

CONTENTS.

Fruit—Scotch—Poor Man's—Neapolitan—Queen of Puddings—Bread—Dandy—Cider—Quaking—Cabinet—Fig—Carrot—Ice—Lemon—Rice. SAUCES.—Sauce—Wine—Pudding Sauce—Another—Mock Cream—Lemon—Farina Jelly Sauce 69-83

PASTRY AND PIES.

Pie Crust—Another—Puff Paste—Mince Meat for Pies—Another—Cocoanut Pie—Eastern Shore Potato—Cream—Another Apple—Lemon Cheesecakes—Cracker Apple—Lemon—Another—Lemon Custard—Raisin—English Apple—Nice—Cheesecakes—Pumpkin—Fruit—Orange Custard—Summer—Mince—Peach Dumplings—Potato—Cherry................,................ 84-90

CAKES.

Remarks on Cake—Vanity—Spice Cakes—Anise-Seed Cakes—Chocolate—Delicate—Rich—Coffee—Ocean—French Loaf—Delicate—Jenny Lind—Cream—Another—Orange—Citron—Measured Pound—Cream Puffs—Another—Chocolate Eclairs—Hickory Nut—Cocoanut—Fruit—Rich Molasses—Marbled—Jelly Roll—White Sponge—Sponge—Crullers—New Year's Cakes—Cake Waffles—Lady—Cocoanut—Hermit's—Jessie—Nameless—Crullers—Spice—Gold and Silver—Cocoanut Drops—Hickory Nut—Sponge—Gingerbread—Kisses—Harrison—Lemon—Coffee—Lady Fingers—Almond—Jelly Cakes—Pound—Watermelon—Brown Stone Front—Mountain Ice—Old Lady—Election—Christmas Cakes—Hard Gingerbread—Aunt Lincoln's—Loaf—Soft Jumbles—Plum—Nut—Delicate—Almond Macaroons—Jelly—Cocoanut Cones—Spice—Feather—Lady—Queen—Jackson Jumbles—Quaker—Walnut—Cream Puffs—Lemon Jelly—Imperial—Sugar Gingerbread—Orange—Snow—Custard—Bims—Molasses—Dried Apple—Lemon—1, 2, 3, 4—Doughnuts—Camp Meeting—Kisses—The Alphistera or Variety—Summer Pound—Jackson—Corn Starch—Cinnamon—Buns—Ginger Snaps—Cream Sponge—Albany—Cinnamon Wafers—Chocolate Cakes—Strawberry Short—Black—Fancy—Leopard—La African—Fig—White Fruit—Soft Waffles—Almond Sand—Molasses—Sponge—Strawberry Short Cake 91-117

PICKLES AND CATSUPS.

Pickles—German Pickles—To Pickle Onions—To Pickle Cauliflower—Cucumber Pickles—To Pickle Peaches, Plums or Pears—Peach Mangoes—Pickled Tomatoes—Tomato Catsup—Another—Pickle Sauce—Chow Chow—Piccalilli—Cucumber Catsup—Walnut Catsup—Cantilope Pickle—Tomato Condiment............118-122

SPICED FRUIT.

Spiced Currants—Spiced Plums—Pickled Peaches—Another—Sweet Pickles—Spiced Cherries........ 123-124

PRESERVES AND JELLIES.

Jelly—Crab Apple Jelly—Currant and Raspberry Jam—Orange Marmalade—Peach Jam—Cherry Sweetmeats—Lemon Jelly—Wine Jelly—Orange Jelly—Marmalade—Fruit Jelly—Brandy Peaches—Lemon Butter—Coffee Jelly—To Make a Hen's Nest—Gelatine Apples—Ambrosia—Strengthening Jelly—Cherry Jam—

Currant Jelly—To Can Peaches—Chipped Pears—Raspberry Jelly—To Preserve Plums—To Cook Apples—Wine Jelly—Calves' Feet Jelly—To Preserve Watermelon Rinds—Fox Grape Jelly—To Preserve Clingstone Peaches—Cranberry Jelly—Ale Jelly—Rule for Canning Fruit—Neapolitan Jelly—Brandy and Preserved Pine-apples..125-134

CUSTARDS, CREAMS, ICES, ETC.

Bavarian Cream—Charlotte Russe—Velvet Cream—Apple Soufflé—Floating Island of Apples—Pistachio Cream—Charlotte Russe—Fairy Apples—Apple Snow—Dutch Flummery—Spanish Cream—Flummery—Almond Custard—Floating Island—Pink Coloring for Icing—Chocolate Icing—Angelic Fodder—Egg Cream—Delmonico Ice Cream—Charlotte Russe—Souffler de Russe—Chocolate Cream—Orange Soufflè—Rice Cups—Chocolate Blanc Mange—Boiled Custard—Cream Glacé - Tapioca Cream—Coffee Custard—Brandy Cream—Caledonia Cream—Carragreen Blanc Mange—Ice Cream—Cream or Boiled Custard—Spanish Cream—Snow and Ice Pudding—Apple Foam—Lemon Cream—Chocolate Custard—Italian Cream—Floating Island—To Whip Cream—A Trifle—Barley Cream—Cream à la Vanilla—Almond Icing—Cream Chocolate—Orange Float—Chocolate Merangue—Chocolate Ice—Lemon Ice..134-146

CANDY.

Chocolate Caramels—White Sugar—Molasses—Maillard's Chocolate Caramels—Cocoanut — Chocolate Cream Drops—Toffy—Cocoanut Cream—Lemon Drops—Chocolate Cream Drops—Walnut Candy—Pop Corn Cakes—Vanilla Caramels—Crystallized Pop Corn...146-148

BEVERAGES.

Mead—Currant Wine—Whipped Cream and Wine—Milk Punch—Cream Soda—Egg-Nog—Pie Plant Wine—Apple Jack—Punch—Lemonade—Gum Arabic Water—Apple Water—Cherry Bounce—Claret Cup..149-152

MISCELLANEOUS.

To Wash Blankets—To Take out Iron Rust—To Clean Gold Chains—Chapped Hands—Flaxseed Poultice—Poultice—Asthma Cure—For Cleaning Silver—To Wash Hair Brush—To Clean a Fine Tooth Comb—An Excellent Wash for the Hair—Java Water—Cologne—Cleaning Gloves—To Remove Grease from Silk—To Cure a Felon—Something Worth Knowing—Insects in Cages—To Wash Navy-blue Woolen Stockings—To Crystallize Grasses and Twigs—Borax for Washing—Polish for Walnut Furniture—Wash for the Hair—Toilet—For Cleaning Paint—To Make Linen Glossy—Tooth Powder—Compress for Sprains—Antidote to Poison—To Stop the Flow of Blood—Eau Sucre—White Liniment—Items for Housekeepers—Earache—For Roaches—Cure for Small-pox and Scarlet Fever—To Clean Marble............. 153-160

DINNER, LUNCH AND TEA......................................161-162

BILLS OF FARE...162-164

RELIABLE COOK BOOK.

SOUPS.

To Make Stock for White Soup and Gravies.

Put two knuckles or shins of veal, two onions, two tablespoonfuls of salt, into eight qts. of water. Boil this six hours ; strain it into a stone jar, and keep it in a cold place. When it is cold, take off the fat.

To Make Stock for Brown Soup.

Take two shins of beef, a shin of veal, eight qts. of water, one doz. cloves, and one doz. pepper-corns. Boil this eight hours; strain it into a stone jar, and when it is cold, remove the fat. This is a very nice stock to use instead of water in making gravies for any kind of dark meat, such as beef, mutton, venison and all kinds of wild fowl.

Corn Soup.

MRS. HULBERT.

Twelve ears of corn cut from the cob, boil corn and cob together in water enough to cover them. Take out most of the corn and add one qt. of milk, boil, half hour, thicken with butter, flour, pepper and salt. Have two eggs well beaten in the soup tureen, pour in the soup, stirring fast all the time.

Wine Soup.

Mrs. C. L. T.

Boil quarter of a lb. of pearl barley or sago in a qt. of water, some stick cinnamon, lemon rind and quarter of lb. of seedless raisins or currants for two hours; sugar to taste, then add one pt. of claret and allow it to boil up once. Fresh ripe cherries can be used in place of the raisins.

Potato Soup.

Mrs. Churchman.

One qt. milk, when boiling add five potatoes cooked and rubbed through a sieve, two onions, add three beaten eggs when boiled up once, butter size of egg, stir well.

Okra Gumbo Soup.

A. W.

One onion cut in small pieces, three lbs. veal cutlet cut in small pieces, one lb. of ham cut in small pieces, fifty okra cut small, one pt. browned flour, two qts. tomatoes stewed, put some lard in a frying-pan, when hot put in the okras and onion, when browned take up, and put in the pan the ham and veal to brown; then stir very gradually on the flour six qts. of boiling water, add the browned veal, ham, okra onion, then add the tomatoes, season very high with red pepper and salt, boil three hours stirring often, strain before serving.

French Soup.

Miss Cripps.

Take a sheep's head and pluck, cut into pieces and boil gently in a gallon of water till reduced to half the quantity; add a small teacupful of pearl barley, an onion, turnips, carrots, a bunch of sweet herbs and a few cloves; thicken with flour rubbed in butter and add a little mushroom ketchup. Boil the head the day before the soup is needed, boiling it sufficiently for the bones to separate.

Tomato Soup.

Miss Ada Maxwell.

Four or five large tomatoes cut up small, into one and one-half pts. of water, stew ten minutes, then add four soda crackers broken up in small pieces, half cup butter, one pt. milk, salt and pepper to taste; let all boil up once.

Tomato Soup No. 2.

Mrs. Churchman.

Two qts. sliced tomatoes, six qts. water, two lbs. beef, boil three hours, tablespoonful butter, season and serve with bits of toast, celery improves it.

Mulligatawny Soup.

Mrs. F. Taylor.

Cut a chicken in small pieces and put in a stew-pan, with a little butter, half a chopped onion, one pt., *very scant*, of curry powder, and let them brown. Then add two qts. of chicken, veal and beef stock; if you have not these use hot water. Let it boil half hour or more, slowly, until it begins to be tender; skim off the fat, and add quarter of a lb. of rice, season with salt and a little pepper. Cook about one hour.

Cream of Spinach Soup.

Mrs. F. Taylor.

Half peck of spinach thoroughly washed, put into a large pot of boiling water with a handful of salt. Cook until tender enough to break in your fingers; drain and chop, then pass it through a coarse sieve. Boil two qts. milk, when boiled stir the spinach into it, and add a tablespoonful of corn starch wet in cold water, and quarter teaspoonful of nutmeg. Cook five minutes and serve hot. Asparagus, lettuce and fresh peas are good in the place of spinach and make a nice soup.

Scotch Broth.

Mrs. F. Taylor.

Take from a shoulder of mutton two lbs. of the lean meat. Cut this with your vegetables in medium size dice shape, using one turnip, one carrot, one small onion. Put into a sauce-pan two ozs. of butter, add the lean meat and brown it; put in a tablespoonful of dry flour and add the vegetables, then fill up the sauce-pan with three qts. of stock and hot water, add half lb. barley which has been soaked in cold water, and season with pepper and salt. Let it simmer one hour.

Crab Soup, very rich.

Fry three onions brown in butter, slice a dozen large tomatoes, and cook together; season with red pepper, salt and nutmeg to your taste; pick out a dozen crabs, add two qts. of water. Simmer until thick.

Noodles for Soup.

Mrs. Thomas.

One cup flour, one egg, eggshellful of water, a little salt; make a hole in the cup of flour, pour in the egg and water; mix very stiff, roll thin, and cut in thin strips.

Black Bean Soup.

Mrs. C. Ide.

Soak one qt. of black beans in one qt. of water over night; boil them in the morning till thoroughly cooked, and then strain through a wire sieve; when ready to prepare the soup for dinner, put over the fire with beef stock, two onions, four whole sticks of celery (the latter to be taken out before serving), salt and pepper; when served, pour in a glass of wine and the whole yolks of several hard boiled eggs. This makes a very delicious soup, both as to taste and appearance.

Cheap Green Pea Soup.

Two qts. of green peas, piece of lean ham, some bones from roast meat, two onions sliced, a few sprigs of parsley, a bunch of sweet herbs. Put them to stew in two qts. of cold water, let simmer gently. When quite tender strain it, and pulp the peas and other vegetables through a sieve. Put it on the fire again, with pepper and salt, and about a pt. of milk. Serve with fried bread cut into small dice.

Strengthening Broth for Invalids.
W. S.

Cut raw beef in squares one inch thick, place in soup-plate with just enough *cold* water to cover the meat, cover with another plate, and allow it to stand twelve hours. Refuse the meat, as it will have then lost all nutriment, heat the blood thus extracted and season with pepper and salt.

Oyster Soup.

One qt. of oysters, separated from the liquor, washed thoroughly in about a pt. of water. Strain the liquor and add one qt. of milk, nutmeg and pepper, with three crackers pounded fine; add quarter of a lb. of butter to the liquor. Boil all together five minutes. Add the oysters and boil a few minutes.

White Soup.

A large knuckle of veal, four qts. of water, a little celery seed, two onions, two carrots, two turnips; boil down to two qts., strain the liquor and let it stand until it is cold. Take off all the fat, add one pt. of new milk or cream, the beaten yolks of three eggs, and a little vermicelli. Let it come to a boil. It is well to prepare the broth the day before it is wanted.

Chicken Soup.

After boiling tender, skim off the fat, and put in a cupful of rice and a head of celery; pepper and salt to taste.

Beef Soup.

Boil a shin of beef the day before it is wanted; if that is not convenient, have the shin cracked up well; put to boil in five or six qts. of water, boil five or six hours, skim it very often; cut up very fine half a white cabbage, chop two turnips, three carrots, and three onions; put them into the soup, with pepper and salt, boil it two hours; half an hour before serving take out bone and gristle. Never hurry soup, the meat should boil long and slowly, and put on in cold water after rubbing it thoroughly with salt to draw out the juice. Skim just before it comes to a boil.

Vermicelli Soup.

Miss C. SHIVELY.

Six lbs. of beef or veal, place in water enough to cover it, and boil until tender; remove the meat, and to three or four qts. of the liquid sprinkle a half lb. of vermicelli, letting the vermicelli boil fifteen or twenty minutes, season with a little salt, when it is ready for the table.

Soup à la Julienne.

MRS. HAXTUN.

Make a gravy soup and strain it before you put in the vegetables, cut some turnips and carrots in ribbons, and some onions and celery into lozenges, boil them separately; when the vegetables are thoroughly boiled, put them in the tureen with the soup, and lay gently on the top some small squares of toasted bread without crust, taking care they do not tumble down and disturb the brightness of the soup.

Calves' Head Soup.
Mrs. Haxtun.

Boil a calf's head, take the water after the head is sufficiently cooked to take the bones out, put it in a stew-pot, then put in a few whole cloves and allspice, season well with pepper and salt; take a tablespoonful of butter and the same of browned flour, mix thoroughly, add thyme, parsley, and two onions, let it boil long and slowly; strain it, return it to the pot, stir in the flour and butter, let it continue boiling; make force-meat balls of veal chopped fine, mix with bread crumbs, season with pepper and salt, fry a light brown; boil two eggs hard, slice them into the tureen, put the fried force-meat balls in and a few slices of lemon, and a cup of wine and catsup mixed. (Walnut is preferable.)

Mock Bisquit Soup.
Miss M. Moore, New York.

Take a can of tomatoes and strain, add a pinch of soda, then in another sauce-pan boil three pts. of milk thickened with a tablespoonful of corn starch mixed with a little cold milk; add butter size of an egg, salt and pepper to taste, mix with tomatoes, let come to a boil and serve.

FISH, OYSTERS, CLAMS, ETC.

Baked Shad.

MRS. THOMAS.

Take a large shad, and fill it with a stuffing of grated bread made with sweet milk, butter, pepper, salt and one egg beaten up. Lay the fish in a pan with a little water and bake an hour, basting with butter and water.

Lobster Salad.

MRS. SILLECK.

Take the meat from the body and claws of a large, well boiled lobster, and mash the coral with a wooden spoon; chop *not very fine*. To one cup of meat use two of chopped celery or lettuce. For dressing use "Durkee's" salad dressing, garnish with eggs and lettuce. Previously to garnishing place salad back in the shell and arrange claws as though it had not been opened.

Pickled Shad, nice relish.

MRS. SILLECK.

Take a large shad cut in about eight pieces, wash well and rub plenty of salt on them, lay them in a stone jar, add twenty pepper-corns, ten whole allspice, ten cloves, a few pieces of whole mace, lump of butter size of an egg, cover with good vinegar, stand it on the back of the range and let it remain twenty-four hours; be sure it does not boil or even simmer.

Bluefish and fresh mackerel are excellent prepared in the same manner, only adding more butter.

Scallops.

Swell them in salt water over night; in the morning dry them on a cloth, dip in egg, then in cracker crumbs, and fry brown.

Scalloped Lobster or Salmon.

S. B. D.

Two ounces of butter put in a saucepan, when melted add one large teaspoon of flour, stir until it becomes yellow, add one cup of milk, stirring till it becomes creamy, salt and pepper to taste. Chop the lobster or salmon fine, stir in till it becomes very hot, then take from the range and add the juice of one lemon. Put in a dish or into the lobster shell, sprinkle on top bread crumbs and a little butter. Place in oven and brown half hour.

Lobster Croquettes.

Mrs. Chandler.

Chop meat fine, mix with salt and pepper. One-fourth part bread crumbs. Make into balls with melted butter, dip in egg, then in bread crumbs. Serve with parsley.

Turbot à la Crème.

Miss Thurston.

For five lbs. of halibut, boil an onion and a bunch of parsley in a pt. of milk. Thicken a pt. of cream with four tablespoonfuls of flour, then take out the onion and parsley and boil the milk and cream together, add a spoonful of butter, a little mace, salt and pepper. The fish must be picked up fine after it is boiled. Then put some of the sauce in the dish, then a layer of fish, alternating until the dish is full. Put fine cracker crumbs on the top and bake.

Fish Cakes.

Mrs. Churchman.

A large salt fish, picked fine, a qt. raw potatoes, put both in cold water and boil until done; when cool, mash with silver fork, butter size of an egg, tablespoonful of milk, two eggs, pepper and salt. When cold, make into cakes, drop into boiling fat, and fry as doughnuts.

Roast Clams.

Mrs. Silleck.

Have a hot fire, remove lids and center piece, place clams, previously washed clean, on top of the coals. When the shells open they are done. Serve in shells.

Scalloped Oysters.

Miss Susie Boyd, Boston.

Grate a stale loaf of bread; crackers will answer, but bread is *much* better. Butter a deep dish, sprinkle in a layer of crumbs with a little salt, pepper and bits of butter, then a layer of oysters with a little liquid and salt, pepper and butter, layer of bread crumbs, one of oysters, seasoning each layer, until the dish is filled, having the crumbs on top, moisten the last layer well. A medium size dish will bake in twenty or thirty minutes.

Fried Oysters.

Miss C. Shively.

Select the largest and drain them well on a cloth, then dip them in rolled crackers; fry in either butter or lard until they are a nice brown, and season with pepper and salt.

Oysters Baked in Shells.

MRS. W. B. KENDALL.

Make a thick batter of flour, milk and butter, cook well in a saucepan. Scald a few small oysters, after which wash in cold water. Drain off the water and mix the oysters with the batter, season with nutmeg, pepper and salt. Put in *clam* shells, sprinkle over with bread crumbs and put a small bit of butter on top. Bake until brown.

Hard-Shell Crabs.

MISS L. PARKER.

Wash them in cold water and put them, alive, in boiling hot water, just enough to cover them. Boil from twenty to thirty minutes with the pot tightly covered. Should be eaten cold.

Soft-Shell Crabs.

MISS L. PARKER.

Wash them clean in cold water, cut out their mouths and lift up the pointed corners of the shell, taking out the "dead men." Flour well, and fry in boiling lard and butter after seasoning.

Scalloped Clams.

M. E. W.

Chop the clams fine, season with pepper and a little salt; mix in another dish some powdered cracker moistened with a little warm milk, part of the juice of the clams, a beaten egg or two, a small spoonful melted butter. Now stir into this the chopped clams; bake in small patty-pans, send to table in tin-pans; or wash, wipe and butter some of the large clam shells, fill them with the mixture and bake.

Stewed Eels.
Miss Cripps.

Two lbs. of eels, one pt. of good stock, one onion, three or four cloves, pieces of lemon-peel, one glass of port or Madeira wine, three tablespoonfuls of cream, a thickening of flour, Cayenne pepper and lemon juice to taste. Wash and skin the eels, cut them in pieces, pepper and salt them and put in a stew-pan with the stock. Add the onion, cloves, lemon-peel and wine. Stew gently for half an hour. Keep the eels hot on a dish, strain the gravy, thicken the cream with a little flour. Mix all together and boil two minutes, having added a little Cayenne and lemon juice. Pour the gravy over the eels and serve.

Jellied Eels.
Mrs. T.

Boil for fifteen minutes six large well-cleaned eels cut in finger-length pieces, in three parts water and one part wine-vinegar, some salt, whole cloves, pepper, three bay leaves and three shallots; drain through a sieve, replace the eels in the liquid, when cold remove the fat, then take out the eels; pour the liquid with the strained jelly of six calves' feet previously boiled, from which the fat has been gathered, allow this to come to a boil; then add the whites of six well-beaten eggs; skim the same, pour several times through a jelly-bag, if not sufficiently sour add the juice of two lemons; pour a quantity of the liquid in a mold, then some sliced lemon, then eels, then liquid, and alternate until all is used; when jellied it is ready for use.

Steamed Oysters.
W. S.

Drain the oysters well, place in pan with large piece of butter, season with salt and pepper, cover closely, shake them occasionally. Toast bread and place on dish nicely; when oysters are cooked, turn on toast and serve immediately.

Frying Fish.

Wash and wipe them perfectly dry, rub over lightly with a little flour, and cover them with bread crumbs and the yolk of an egg; then place in a pan of boiling dripping or lard sufficient to completely cover them, and when done place on a dish before the kitchen fire. The most inexperienced hand will thus be able to send them to table crisp and of a beautiful brown color; but if the fat be insufficient or not quite hot when the fish is put in the pan, they will be flabby and greasy. Too small quantity of fat is the common error.

To Broil Mackerel.

Clean and split them open, wipe dry, lay them on a clean gridiron, rubbed with suet, over a very clear slow fire; turn; season with pepper and salt and a little butter.

Oyster Pie.

MRS. THOMAS.

One hundred oysters; pick them out carefully and strain the liquor. Put them on to plump in their own liquor, then take them off and season with pounded mace, cloves, pepper and salt if required, season to taste. Three hard boiled yolks of eggs cut up fine with a slice of grated bread crumbs, mix well and strew over the tops of the oysters, and about two ozs. of butter cut into small bits. Put the crust on and bake in a quick oven.

Boiled Salmon.

Salmon should be well cleansed but not soaked in water; rub a little salt into the body, flour a cloth and pin it up, and put it into boiling water. For a piece weighing six lbs., after it begins to boil, let boil about half an hour. Serve it with drawn butter and eggs or fish sauce.

Fish Chowder ("Com. Stevens.")

MRS. OATMAN.

Four tablespoonfuls of onion fried with pork, one qt. boiled potatoes well mashed, one pilot bread and a half, broken, one tablespoonful summer savory and thyme, mixed, quarter bottle of catsup, half bottle of port or claret wine, half a nutmeg, grated, half a teaspoon each of cloves, mace and allspice, one teaspoonful red pepper, three teaspoonfuls black pepper, salt, six lbs. of bass or cod cut in slices. Put the whole in a kettle together, with water enough to cover two or three inches. Boil one and a half hours, stirring gently.

Fried Smelts.

Split them just far enough to clean them, lay them in salt and water for one hour, wash, clean and wipe them dry. Have ready two eggs well beaten in a plate, and some cracker crumbs in another plate. Put two lbs. of lard into the frying-pan, set it on the fire until very hot, dip the smelts into the egg, roll them in the crumbs and put into the boiling fat. Fry a light brown; serve with drawn butter.

Pickled Oysters.

MRS. DUCKER.

Boil the oysters nearly done, then drain on a dish until cold. Add juice and vinegar according to taste, whole peppers and cloves. For six hundred oysters slice six lemons very thin; put the lemons in the day they are to be used. Don't make them too sour with vinegar, it is apt to cut them; add salt.

Pickled Clams.

Add whole pepper, cloves, mace and vinegar to boiled clams.

Pickled Oysters.

MRS. SILLECK.

Buy fine large oysters, take them out of their liquor, lay them in a kettle, sprinkle well with salt, pour boiling water over them, and allow them just to come to a boil. Have ready a pan of *ice* water with a lump of ice remaining in it, take oysters out of the hot and place them *immediately* in ice water; this process makes them white and plump; when cool, spread on marble or between cloths dipped in cold water, boil and strain the liquor; with every pt. add one pt. of good vinegar, one gill of lemon juice, a few blades of mace, one tablespoonful of whole cloves, same of whole black pepper; let it boil, and pour over the oysters while boiling hot.

Clam Fritters.

MRS. WARD.

Drain thoroughly twenty-five middle-sized clams. Beat up with four or five eggs, fry in equal parts of butter and lard.

Cream Fish, splendid.

MRS. HAXTUN.

Two lbs. of haddock or rock fish, a pt. of cream, an eighth of a lb. of butter, a tablespoonful of flour. Put a little salt in the water and boil your fish well; when done skin it, take out all the bones and flake it with a fork. Then take your cream or very rich milk and boil it, and after beating your butter and flour to a cream, stir it in the hot cream, which must be seasoned,. and if you like put the heart of a small onion in it. You then butter a dish and put a layer of fish and one of dressing until the dish is filled, but be sure to make the dressing come last. Cover the whole with a layer of bread crumbs and bake in the oven.

Potted Shad.

MRS. DOUBLEDAY.

Clean the shad and cut it in small pieces, put it in a small stone crock, and sprinkle with whole peppers, salt and mace; fill the jar with vinegar, cover over with a piece of muslin and bread dough, and bake in a very moderate oven twenty-four hours. The bones will be found entirely dissolved.

Stewed Terrapin.

MRS. HAXTUN.

Boil the terrapins. In opening the animals save the juice that comes from them. Sprinkle with Cayenne pepper and salt that have been previously mixed, put on the fire some cream with butter and flour nicely mixed, boil, then put in the terrapins, boil again without boiling to pieces. Put wine in just before serving.

Clam Chowder.

MRS. WALZ.

To fifty medium sized clams add one gallon of cold water. Stand them over the fire until the shells open, then take them up and chop them fine, add to the water in which the clams were boiled one lb. of salt pork cut in small pieces, about one dozen good sized potatoes, then tomatoes, onions and seasoning to taste. Place in dish with alternate layers of bread crumbs, having chopped clams for top layer.

MEATS.

Filet of Veal.

Remove the bone; fill the cavity with dressing, made same as for *Turkey*. Skewer the veal tight, to keep the dressing in. Make deep incisions all over the surface of the meat and fill closely with the dressing; baste often. A piece weighing eight lbs. requires about three hours to bake. Pickled *Ham* with the bone removed is excellent baked in the same manner.

Sweetbreads.

Soak in salt and water. Fry them a nice brown; season with Cayenne pepper and salt. For the gravy, half a teacup of the thin part of cooked tomatoes, two tablespoonfuls of wine; thicken with butter and flour, season with cloves, pepper and salt.

Roast Beef.

Wash the joint and wipe thoroughly; place in oven; remember never to season meat until it begins to brown. Then dredge with salt, pepper and flour, and baste often. When done place on a hot dish. To the gravy remaining in the pan add one gill of water, a little flour, pepper and salt.

For *Roast Lamb and Mutton*—see Roast Beef.

Corned Mutton.

MISS MOFFAT.

Two small cups of salt, a little lump of saltpeter, one teaspoonful of sugar. Boil three hours.

Stuffed Lamb.

Mrs. Thomas.

From three to four lbs. breast or fore-quarter of lamb. Wash with cold water, rub well with salt inside and out. Stuff with a dressing made of dry bread, pepper, salt, butter and a little hot water. Sprinkle with pepper, salt and flour and bake in a quick oven about two hours.

To Corn Beef.

Mrs. L. Thomas.

Put salt in cold water until it will bear up an egg, and add about one tablespoonful of brown sugar. Leave some salt in the bottom of a stone crock. Rub your beef well with dry salt and put it in the brine with a weight to keep it under; a piece of the brisket or cross rib is best. It takes from three days to one week, according to size.

Sugar-Cured Ham, Virginia Style.

Mrs. J. Moore.

Ham one year old, ten to fourteen lbs., half hour to a lb., simmer in warm water. Keep until cold, then skin. Spread over top of ham one egg beaten with large tablespoonful of brown sugar, two of vinegar, one small teaspoonful of dry mustard and thickened with cracker-dust. Sprinkle with vinegar. Bake one hour. Baste constantly one hour with its own essence.

Ham, Hartford Club.

Mrs. J. Moore.

Soak ham four days, changing the water twice a day. Then put on to simmer four hours in cider and a handful of new-mown hay. After it is done take off the skin and pour sherry or claret over it, and a little fine sugar. Then brown in the oven.

Baked Ham.
Mrs. W. B. Kendall.

Soak the ham twenty-four hours in cold water. Make a paste of flour and water, stiff enough to roll. Cover the ham entirely, bone and all, with the paste. Put in a pan, on two or three muffin-rings or anything that will keep it an inch or so from the bottom of the pan. Bake in a hot oven. A twelve-lb. ham requires four hours' baking. The paste forms a hard crust around the ham, and the skin comes off with it.

Spiced Beef.
Miss Mecham.

Three lbs. beef chopped fine, three eggs well beaten, one tablespoon milk, one of salt, one teaspoonful pepper, cloves and nutmeg to taste, two soda-crackers powdered, mix all well together, cover with pieces of butter, baste well. Bake one hour and a quarter. Then press with weight, cut cold in slices.

Dish for Tea.
Mrs. Churchman.

One lb. of beef, one lb. of veal chopped, boil in a very little water, when done season. Put into a mold, cut in slices when cold.

Stewed Beef.
S. B. D.

Put a piece of butter size of an egg into a pan, when very hot have ready a choice piece of solid meat and put in raw and let it fry until nice and brown, then pour over a pt. of water and cover tight and let cook two hours or until done. Have nice *little* onions or carrots cooked separately (or with it), and cut in slices and put on the meat just before taking up, wet a little flour and mix into your gravy, cook a minute or so and pour over the whole.

Pressed Tongue or Ham.

Mrs. Silleck.

Remains of tongue and ham chopped fine, with this mix a little made mustard. Have ready one cup of gelatine prepared without sweetening, after wetting mold with cold water, pour in first a little gelatine, lay on top of this sliced lemons and hard boiled eggs, so that your design may be visible when turned out. Then add layer of meat, then gelatine, and so on till the mold is full.

Force Meat Balls, nice.

Miss L. Middleton.

Mix with one lb. of chopped veal (other meat can be used) one egg, a little butter or raw pork chopped fine, one cup of bread crumbs, the water from stewed meat, season with salt and pepper, make into small balls and fry brown.

Beef's Heart.

If not already open, cut it on the side, boil about fifteen or twenty minutes; then fill with nice dressing and bake until tender.

Kidney Omelette.

Remove all skin, fat and sinew from a fresh kidney, whether sheep's or calf's. Cut it small, season well, fry in hot butter. Beat six eggs together with a glassful of white wine; heat a little butter in a frying-pan, pour in the eggs, and before they are regularly set place the kidney in the middle; turn in the ends of the omelette and serve; garnish with thin slices of lemon.

Venison Steaks.

Season with pepper and salt. When the gridiron has been well heated over a bright bed of coals, grease the bars, and lay the steaks upon it. Broil them well, turning only once, and taking care to save as much of the gravy as possible. Serve with currant jelly laid on each steak.

To make Croquettes.

Take cold fowl or fresh meat of any kind, with slices of ham, fat or lean; chop together very fine, add half as much stale bread grated, some salt, pepper, nutmeg, a teaspoonful of made mustard, tablespoon of catsup and a lump of butter; knead all well together until it resembles sausage meat; make up in cakes or balls size of a walnut, dip in yolks of eggs (beaten), cover thickly with grated bread and fry a light brown.

To Boil Corned Beef.

Wash it thoroughly and put in a pot that will hold plenty of water. The water should be *boiling;* the same care is necessary in skimming it as for fresh meat. Allow half an hour to every lb. of meat after it has commenced to boil. Much depends on its being boiled gently and long. If to be eaten cold, lay it when boiled into a coarse earthen dish or pan, and over it a piece of board size of the meat. Upon this put a clean stone or a couple of flat-irons. Salt meat is much improved by being pressed; it presents a marble-like appearance.

Baked Calves' Liver.

S. P. F.

Take a calf's liver, season very highly with pepper and salt, lay thin slices of salt pork over it; put in a dripping-pan with some water, set in the oven to bake, baste occasionally with a little butter, bake for one hour and a half, serve with the gravy from the pan.

Meat Loaf.
Mrs. J. Raymond.

One and a half lbs. of raw veal or beef, one quarter lb. salt pork, one lb. grated bread crumbs, three eggs, quarter lb. of butter. Season very high with pepper and salt, bake in a loaf and eat when cold, if salt pork is not liked, use two lbs. of meat, and instead of bread use eight small butter crackers (rolled), four eggs and a little more than half a cup of butter. A little nutmeg is an improvement.

An Excellent Stew.
Mrs. Voorhies.

Two and a half lbs. of mutton cut in small pieces, nine potatoes and two onions sliced thin; one and a half cups of flour and half a cup of lard or suet, rubbed together, as for pastry. Put a layer of mutton in bottom of sauce-pan, then a layer of potatoes and onions, with salt, pepper, thyme, and sage to taste, then a layer of mutton, etc. Cover the last layer with the flour. Close tightly and set where it will cook slowly for two hours. The steam and fat make moisture.

Ham and Chicken Pie.
Marion Harland.

Cut up and parboil a tender young chicken. Line a deep dish with good pie-crust. Cut some thin slices of cold boiled ham and spread a layer next the crust, then arrange pieces of fowl on the ham. Cover this in turn with slices of hard-boiled eggs, butter and pepper. Proceed in this order until your materials are used up, then pour in enough veal or chicken gravy to prevent dryness. Unless you have put in too much water for the size of the fowl, the liquor in which the chicken was boiled is best for this purpose. Bake one hour and a quarter for a large pie.

Veal Palé.

S. B. D.

Three and a half lbs. of the finest part of a leg of veal chopped fine; six crackers rolled fine; two eggs well beaten; piece of butter size of an egg; good slice of salt pork chopped fine, one tablespoon of salt, one teaspoonful of pepper, one grated nutmeg; mix all well together, then put in a dripping pan with a little water; press into a long shaped loaf, cover with rolled cracker, adding small bits of butter thickly over it. Bake two hours, basting often.

Nice Way of Using Cold Meat.

Mrs. Silleck.

Take any kind of cold meat you may happen to have in the house, chop it, season well with salt and pepper, butter a baking dish, have ready some mashed potatoes, put first a layer of meat, adding a little butter or stock if you have it, then a layer of potatoes, next meat, proceed in this manner until dish is full. Let the last layer be of potatoes, strew small lumps of butter over it and bake brown.

Lamb Stew.

Miss C. Shively.

Four lbs. of the fore-quarter of lamb, cut up in small pieces, boiled until tender in water enough to cover it, when done season with pepper, salt, butter and a little thickening made of flour and water. Take bread and toast it a nice brown, then cut it into squares and cover the platter with it, then turn the stew over it. Cold meat left from the day before may be used.

Collared Pork.

MRS. TAYLOR.

A leg of fresh pork, two tablespoonfuls powdered sage, two of sweet marjoram, quarter of an oz. of mace powdered, half oz. cloves, two nutmegs, one bunch pot-herbs, chopped fine, a loaf of stale bread, grated fine, half lb. butter, two eggs, one tablespoonful salt, pepper to taste. Mix all with grated bread and egg, take out the bone of the leg of pork, rub the meat on both sides well with salt, spread the seasoning thick in the hole made by taking out the bone, and tie up tightly and in good shape, and skewer well, put in a dripping-pan with water and bake two hours, basting well.

Ropa Alieja.

MRS. HAXTUN.

Take a piece of the boiled shin of beef, cut it small and flour it well. Fry in butter, add a sliced onion and cover with tomatoes. The secret of making this delicious is to boil the meat to rags, and reducing the liquor as nearly as possible to a jelly around it.

Roast Sweetbreads.

MRS. HAXTUN.

Take four fine sweet-breads, trim and parboil them, lay them in cold water till cool, afterward dry them with a cloth. Put some butter in a saucepan, melt and skim it, when clean take it off, skewer each sweet-bread and fasten them on a spit, then glaze them over with beaten eggs and sprinkle with bread crumbs, spread on some of the clarified butter, and then another coat of crumbs. Roast before a clear fire at least quarter of an hour. Have ready some nice veal gravy flavored with lemon juice, and pour it round the sweet-breads before sending to the table.

Calves' Head Pie.

Mrs. Haxtun.

Boil the head one hour and a half, or rather more; after dining from it cut the remaining meat off in slices, boil the bones in a little of the liquor for three hours, then strain it off, and let it remain till the next day. To make the pie, boil two eggs hard and put in the pie with alternate layers of meat, eggs, jelly and chopped lemon. Season with pepper and cover over with bread crumbs or rich crust and bake it.

Beefsteak.

Purchase either porterhouse or tenderloin half an inch thick. The gridiron must be hot and well greased when the steak is placed on it, when nicely browned on one side turn it over, watch carefully that it does not burn, do not stick your fork into the center of the steak as so much juice will be wasted. Season with pepper and salt and butter, and place in oven a few minutes before serving.

Veal Olives.

Mrs. Haxtun.

Cut large slices from a leg of veal, put a layer of force-meat and one of stuffing made of bread, butter and egg, then roll them up tight and tie them, and cover them with bread crumbs, put them in an oven and put onions, salt and pepper with a few cloves, when done make a rich gravy.

For Curing Beef.

Mrs. Haxtun.

To eight gals. of water add two lbs. of brown sugar, one qt. of molasses, four ozs. niter, and fine salt till it will float an egg. This is enough for two common quarters of beef. Has been repeatedly tried and found very fine.

Larded Sweetbreads.
Mrs. Haxtun.

Half boil them, then lay them in cold water, prepare a forcemeat of grated bread, lemon-peel, butter, salt, pepper and nutmeg mixed with beaten yolk of an egg. Cut open the sweetbreads, stuff them, and fasten them up with a skewer or pack-thread, have ready some slips of bacon fat and slips of lemon-peel, cut as fine as small straws, lard the sweet-breads in alternate rows of bacon and lemon-peel, do it regularly, then put them in a Dutch oven and bake them brown. Serve with veal gravy, add a glass of Madeira and the yolk of an egg at the last.

Beef à la Mode.

Round of beef weighing six lbs., make a stuffing of bread, sweet-herbs, pepper, salt, cloves and allspice, cut holes in the meat and fill. Tie in a cloth and stew gently two hours with only enough water to cover it. Then place it in a dripping-pan, with some of the liquor it was stewed in, put in the oven, baste often and bake two hours. Serve with gravy around it.

Yorkshire Pudding.

Three-fourths of a pt. of flour, three eggs, one and a half pts. milk, pinch of salt, one and a half teaspoonfuls Royal Baking Powder. Sift the flour and powder together, add the eggs, beaten with the milk, stir quickly into a rather thinner batter than for griddle cake, pour it in a dripping pan *well buttered ;* rest the meat on skewers two inches above the pudding, allowing the juice to drip on it; if not enough fat on the meat to prevent its burning, place small pieces of butter on it.

French Cutlets.
Mrs. Hobart.

Dip cutlets first in beaten raw egg, then in bread crumbs, fry in *hot* lard. (Have the chops trimmed by the butcher.)

To Dress a Pig's Head.
Mrs. Haxtun.

Boil the head, liver, lights and feet till done, chop them very fine, make a brown gravy with butter, pepper, salt, and allspice to your taste, add a little wine, mix it well with the mince, and put that and the feet round the head and bake it brown.

Curried Dishes.
Mrs. Haxtun.

Veal and chicken are the best for curry. Boil the meat till tender, and separate the joints. Put a little butter in the stew-pan with the chickens, pour on a part of the liquor in which the meat was boiled, nearly enough to cover it, and let it stew twenty minutes more. Prepare the curry thus: for four lbs. of meat, one tablespoonful curry powder, one teacup boiled rice, one tablespoonful flour, same of melted butter, teacup of liquor, half teaspoon of salt, mix and pour over the meat, and let it stew ten minutes more. Boiled rice as an accompaniment.

Stewed Tripe.
Mrs. W. Kendall.

Tripe cut in small pieces, two onions cut in slices, and fried in half a lb. of lard. Put in the tripe, and cook a little and then add one cup vinegar, one bowl beef broth, salt, pepper, three tablespoonfuls flour. Let the whole stew about fifteen minutes.

Ham Sandwiches.

Chop the ham rather fine, season with made mustard, a *little* butter and pepper. Cut very thin slices of (sandwich) bread, take off the crust, butter each slice, lay on dressed ham, and cover with another slice. Turkey chopped and seasoned with pepper, salt and celery seed are very nice.

To Bake a Pig.

Take a pig four or five weeks old, have the butcher clean it thoroughly, fill it with a stuffing made of onions, sage and bread crumbs, sew up and tie the feet, place a stick of wood in the mouth to keep it open, put in pan well buttered, with a little water, butter the pig to prevent its blistering; it will require about three hours to bake. When done take out the wood and put an ear of corn in its mouth. Skim off the fat from the dish it was baked in, and some good gravy will remain at the bottom. Add a little butter rolled in flour and boil it up with the brains, pour it into a dish and serve.

Beef à la Royal.

Take all the bones out of a brisket of beef, and make holes in it about an inch apart. Fill one hole with fat bacon, a second with chopped parsley and a third with chopped oysters. Season these stuffings with pepper, salt, and nutmeg. When the beef is stuffed, put it into a pan, pour over it a pt. of wine boiling hot, dredge well with flour and place in oven, let it remain three hours, when taken out skim off fat, put the meat into your dish and strain the gravy over it. Garnish with pickles.

POULTRY, GAME, ETC.

Boned or Pressed Turkey.

MRS. SILLECK.

One knuckle of veal weighing two lbs., one slice of lean ham, one shallot or onion, sprig of thyme, parsley and celery, one carrot, ten pepper-corns, and one teaspoonful of salt, three pts. cold water, boil all these gently until the liquor is reduced to one pt., then strain without squeezing and let stand until next day, it will then be a firm jelly; scrape off every particle of fat. One package of gelatine soaked in one pt. of cold water half an hour, two tablespoonfuls lemon juice and one of currant jelly dissolved in cold water, nearly one qt. boiling water poured over the gelatine, stir softly, add the jellied stock, then lemon, etc., stir all together, and strain through a flannel bag, have ready four or five hard boiled eggs. The remains of cold roasted or boiled turkey, chicken, beef or veal, jointly or alone, chopped not too fine and well seasoned with celery; *Charlotte Russe* pans are nice to use; dip in cold water, do not wipe; when the jelly begins to congeal, pour a very thin layer in your pan, cut the whites of your eggs in pretty shapes, arrange them on this lower stratum of jelly; if you desire you can add sliced lemon, pickle, etc. Pour in a little more jelly, then a layer of meat, another of jelly, proceed until you have used up all your meat, last layer must be jelly. Set in a cool place, when cold turn out on a flat dish, garnish with parsley or lettuce. You will have a dish as pleasing to the eye as to the palate.

Chicken Salad.

Mrs. J. Hebert.

The white meat of a cold boiled or roasted chicken or turkey, three-quarters the same bulk of chopped celery, two hard-boiled eggs, one raw egg well beaten, one teaspoonful of salt, one of pepper, one of made mustard, three of salad oil, two of white sugar and half a teaspoonful of vinegar. Mince the meat well, removing every scrap of gristle and skin; cut the celery into bits half an inch long or less, mix them and set aside in a cold place while you prepare the dressing. Rub the yolks of the eggs to a fine powder, add the salt, pepper and sugar, then the oil, grinding hard and putting in but a few drops at a time. The mustard comes next, and let all stand together while you whip the raw egg to a froth. Beat this into the dressing, and pour in the vinegar spoonful by spoonful, whipping the dressing well as you do it. Sprinkle a little dry salt over the meat and celery, toss it up lightly with a silver fork, pour the dressing over it, tossing and mixing until the bottom of the mass is as well saturated as the top; turn into the salad bowl and garnish with white of egg (boiled) cut into rings or flowers and sprigs of bleached celery tops. If you cannot get celery, substitute crisp white cabbage, and use celery vinegar in the dressing. You can also in this case chop some green pickles, gherkins, mangoes or cucumbers and stir in.

Chicken Salad.

Mrs. Titus.

Boil a chicken, when cold cut in small bits; cut the white part of a bunch of celery into small pieces. For dressing rub the yolks of hard-boiled eggs smooth, and to each yolk half a teaspoon of mustard, some suet, one tablespoon sweet oil and a wine-glass of vinegar; mix the chicken and celery in a dish and pour the dressing over just before using.

Choosing Fowl.

Select a goose with a clean and white skin, plump breast, and yellow feet, if these latter are red the bird is old. *Turkey.*—If the bird has been long killed, the eyes will appear sunk, and the feet very dry; if fresh the contrary will be the case.

Boned Chicken.

S. B. D.

Boil one chicken till it falls in pieces, boil with it a small piece of *lean* salt pork. Take the meat off the bones, pound the bones, and put them back into the liquor in which the chicken was boiled; add a pinch of gelatine (after dissolving it); when ready for the molds, cut hard-boiled eggs in pieces and place on the bottom and sides of the molds; the meat the same, white and dark alternating. Fill the mold with the liquor strained.

Chicken Croquettes.

S. B. D.

Take cold veal or chicken, chop fine, and about one-third cold ham chopped fine; pepper, nutmeg and salt to taste; make quite thin by adding milk, make stiff again with rolled cracker, add melted butter and a little chopped parsley, roll in balls, dip in egg and cracker dust and fry in boiling lard.

Potted Pigeon.

After picking, drawing and washing well, cut off the pinions, dry well with a cloth, season with pepper and salt, roll a lump of butter in chopped parsley and put it into the pigeons, sew them up, place in a pot, cover them with butter, bake in a moderately heated oven; when done, put them in potting pots and pour clarified butter over them. Keep in a dry place.

Potage à la Reine.
Mrs. Taylor.

Put one chicken, one pound of rice, three cloves and a small onion, one carrot, in cold water enough to cover them, adding a little salt. Boil three and a half hours slowly; the chicken should boil up and skim it before you put in the vegetables. Strain through a sieve. Pound the white meat of the chicken and press that through a coarse sieve. Add veal stock or chicken stock if you have them; but if you have neither, add boiling water; season with pepper, salt and nutmeg. After you have prepared it thus you must not put it over the fire only as you place it in a pan of hot water, else it will curdle. Add half pt. of cream or rich milk.

Jellied Chicken.
Mrs. H. Forker.

Boil a pair of chickens, covering them entirely with water; boil till the meat falls from the bone, put it on a dish to cool, leaving the bones to boil about twenty minutes longer; strain the liquid and let it cool. Next morning cut the chicken in pretty small pieces, take the fat from the jelly, warm the jelly, season it with salt, black pepper, a little mace and allspice; add two tablespoonfuls of walnut catsup and one or two of Worcestershire sauce. Stir the chicken in the liquor while hot; line the bowl with slices of hard-boiled egg and sliced lemon, eight eggs to a pair of chickens; cool in a refrigerator. If more jelly is required dissolve a little of Cox's gelatine.

Stewed Pigeons.
Mrs. Wilder.

Slice eight onions and fry in butter a nice brown, clean pigeons whole; put in each little salt, pepper, thyme and parsley; take the onions from the butter, fry the birds a nice brown, add water and the onions, thicken and stew them about one hour and a half or two hours.

Quail on Squab Pie.

Mrs. Sumner.

Half doz. birds, one and a half lbs. steak cut thick, half lb. salt fat pork, six sprigs of parsley, two onions. Put pepper and salt inside each bird, cut the steak into dice, one inch square or less; chop the pork, onions and parsley fine, separately. Line the sides of a deep dish with paste; put the steak in the bottom of the dish, with pepper and salt to taste; then the birds, the pork, the onions and the parsley in layers in the order named. Fill with water, cover with paste, and bake from one to one and a half hours.

Prairie Chicken.

Mrs. Parrott, Keokuk.

Fill the birds with bread or potato stuffing, and roast same as other fowl.

Quail.

Mrs. Parrott, Keokuk.

Stuff them with oysters, or some prefer chestnuts, boiled, peeled and mashed and used for stuffing instead of oysters. Another way to cook quail.—Split them open at the back and broil them, the inside must invariably be broiled first. Serve on toast.

Fried Chicken.

Mrs. Haxtun.

Cut the chicken up one hour before cooking and lay it in salt and water, fry in lard with a little butter, after dipping in a batter made of two eggs, flour, pepper and nutmeg. Make a gravy of half a cup of cream, butter, pepper and nutmeg, put the gravy in the pan after the lard is poured off and let it boil. Dredge in flour.

A Fricassee of Chicken.

MRS. SILLECK.

Cut a pair of chickens into pieces, place in stew-pan with water enough to cover them (cold water), let them boil till tender, season with pepper and salt. The gravy or sauce—Two teaspoonfuls flour, mixed with cold water, to make it like a thin batter, stir until free from lumps, add to it half a pt. of boiling milk and quarter of a lb. of butter. Have ready toasted bread on a platter, place the chicken on this; pour the gravy over the whole and serve.

Baked Turkey.

MRS. TAYLOR.

Put the turkey in a baking-pan (after it is cleaned, stuffed and trussed), with half cup of cold water; baste often and when about half done season well with pepper and salt and butter, also dredge with flour; requires about two hours to bake a turkey. Serve with cranberry sauce.

Chicken Pot Pie.

MRS. HOBART.

Cut the chicken small, with some thin slices of salt pork, cover with cold water, boil until tender, turn it out in a dish, grease your vessel well, then alternate layers of sliced raw potatoes with the chicken, using plenty of seasoning, salt and pepper; make a soda-biscuit crust (about one qt. of flour makes plenty), with very little shortening; line the sides of vessel, cover the top with a crust about half an inch thick, cutting a hole in the middle. Pour the broth over with enough boiling water to cover; boil about ten minutes, then slide it in the oven and bake until brown (about ten minutes), thicken the gravy with flour. Veal done the same way is excellent.

Boiled Turkey.

MRS. HAXTUN.

Make a stuffing of chopped bread and butter, cream, oysters and yolks of eggs. Sew it in and dredge flour over the turkey; put it to boil in cold water, with a spoonful of salt in it, and enough water to cover well, simmer for two hours and a half, less time if small; skim while boiling. It will present a better appearence if wrapped in a cloth dredged with flour; serve with drawn butter, in which put some oysters. Always draw poultry six hours before cooking, or longer.

SALADS AND SAUCES.

Carrot Salad.
Mrs. Voorhis.

Take four large carrots, one onion, handful of parsley, a small head of lettuce; boil the carrots and slice them or cut in small pieces if preferred, the onion chop raw, with part of the parsley or lettuce, leaving the other part for the side of the salad bowl; boil one egg and rub it to paste, then add teaspoonful salt, half teaspoonful of pepper, heaping teaspoonful mustard and three of oil or butter, cup of vinegar; mix all together and serve in salad bowl.

Lettuce Salad.
Mrs. Thomas.

Chop three heads of white lettuce, rub the yolks of two hard-boiled eggs to a powder and add one teaspoonful of white sugar, one of pepper, one half teaspoon salt, same of made mustard and teaspoonful of salad oil; let it stand five minutes, then beat in four tablespoonfuls vinegar. Put the lettuce in a bowl and add the dressing thus made, tossing it through with a fork. Decorate with the whites of the boiled eggs and put a piece of ice in the bottom of your bowl.

Dressing for Chopped White Cabbage.
Half cup vinegar, half cup cold water, small piece of butter; let boil, beat one egg and stir into it; take one teaspoonful of mustard, one of flour, half teaspoon of salt, a pinch of sugar, stir into the boiling vinegar, and let boil a few minutes. Pour over the cabbage and let cool before eating.

Cold Slaw.

Miss Sweet.

For one cabbage take two eggs, half a cup of vinegar, piece of butter size of an egg; beat eggs up light, pour vinegar over eggs, heat the butter and then pour eggs and vinegar into it. Let it cook till it thickens, stirring all the time; when cooked pour it hot over the cold cabbage, which must be nicely cut; add a little salt and pepper, sprinkle on it.

Mint Sauce.

Mrs. Thomas.

Two cents' worth of spear mint, chopped fine; add sugar, vinegar and a little cold water.

Pepper Sauce.

Mrs. Thomas.

One large head of cabbage cut fine, about twenty-five cents' worth of celery, also cut fine; half a dozen small red peppers cut fine, half a dozen green peppers and three or four carrots, also cut fine; mix well together and season with salt, ground mustard and mustard seed; pour over cold vinegar enough to cover it.

Chili Sauce.

Mrs. Sumner.

Nine big tomatoes chopped fine, two large green peppers (take out seeds), one onion, chop together. Two cups vinegar, one and a half tablespoonfuls salt, one tablespoonful brown sugar, one teaspoonful nutmeg, one of cloves, one of cinnamon, one of ginger, one of allspice. Boil one and a half hours.

Hot Slaw.

One head of red cabbage cut fine; place in a porcelain kettle one cup of vinegar, two tablespoonfuls butter, pepper and salt to taste. Simmer fifteen minutes.

Sauce for Mushroom Pâtés.
S. B. D.

A piece of butter size of a lemon, melted slowly; stir in afterward a heaping tablespoonful of flour until quite creamy; add salt and pepper to taste, then a little milk. adding last half a pt. of real cream until it thickens on the fire. It can be put aside until time to cook the mushrooms in the sauce, which should only be for a few minutes; warm the pâtés in the oven and pour the sauce and mushrooms in.

Mayonnaise Sauce.
Mrs. Ruland.

Mix in a two-qt. bowl, to allow room for beating, one even teaspoonful ground mustard and one of salt, with one and a half of vinegar; beat in the yolk of a raw egg, then add gradually from the measure, holding it in the left hand, half a pt. of pure olive oil; pour it in the smallest thread-like stream while with the other hand the beating is brisk and uninterrupted. The mixture will become a very thick batter. Flavor with vinegar or fresh lemon juice.

Egg Sauce for Fish.
Miss Sweet.

One quarter of a lb. of butter mixed with three tablespoonfuls of flour, stir into a pt. of water ; chop three hard-boiled eggs, season with salt, pepper and parsley ; boil until thick.

Chicken Salad Dressing.

Mrs. Ide.

Four eggs, small teaspoonful mustard, half a teaspoon of salt, same of Cayenne pepper, or less if hot dressing is not liked; half a teacupful of sweet oil, one to two tablespoonfuls vinegar, one of cream or milk, piece of butter size of a walnut, boil three eggs hard; when cold mash the yolks with butter, mustard, salt and pepper till they are smooth and light; add a little of the oil as you mash, which will make it easier, add cream, open the other egg, separating the yolk from white; throw the yolk into a bowl and beat with a fork till it becomes thick, then add few drops at a time, mix the oil, beating all the while. If properly done it will become thick like paste; then pour in the vinegar and beat thoroughly, mix the two finally well together. This dressing will keep for a week, the oil never separating. If it is a little too thick thin the cream or milk, but do it carefully. This amount is generally sufficient for three and a half lbs. of chicken and celery. Should the oil be put in too fast or too much at a time it becomes thin, and does not become thoroughly incorporated with the egg.

Oyster Stuffing for Poultry.

Two doz. oysters, strain the liquor off, add one pt. of bread crumbs, two ozs. of butter, season with pepper, salt and mace; wet the stuffing with the liquor from oysters and stuff the bird.

Essence of Celery.

Mrs. Haxtun.

Steep an oz. of celery seed in half a pt. of vinegar. A few drops of this gives a fine flavor to soup and sauce for fowls.

Stuffing for Turkey.

Take a loaf of bread (cut the crust off), soak it in water, when thoroughly soaked squeeze dry, add one onion chopped fine, one egg, season with pepper, salt and summer savory.

Goose Stuffing.

Slice of pork (chopped), two large onions, bread crumbs and a teaspoonful each of pepper, salt and sage. Potatoes may be used if preferred to bread. To destroy the fishy taste of *wild duck* (for which this stuffing may also be used), parboil them with a carrot cut in pieces in each, after which remove the carrot and stuff.

Drawn Butter.

Four ozs. of butter, two tablespoonfuls flour, mix the flour with one pt. of water to a smooth paste, place on the stove in a saucepan, adding the butter and salt to taste; boil three minutes, stirring one way that it may not become lumpy. Capers may be added to this sauce; cut them, do not chop, and add one half teaspoon of pepper and some anchovy essence.

Potato Salad.

Boil a doz. large potatoes, peel them, and when nearly cold slice thin or chop, add two large onions (raw) chopped, salt and pepper to taste, one cup vinegar, half cup melted butter or four tablespoonfuls of salad oil.

Anchovy Sauce.

Put an anchovy into half a pt. of gravy, with a quarter of a lb. of butter rolled in a little flour, stir together until it boils; you may add at your discretion a little lemon juice, red wine or walnut liquor.

Caper Sauce.

Take some capers, chop half of them very fine and put the rest in whole; chop also some parsley with a little grated bread and some salt, put them into butter melted very smooth, let them boil up and then pour it into your sauce-boat.

EGGS.

Omelette.
MRS. A. D. FRENCH, M.D.

Take the yolks of six eggs, beat them light, have ready one even teaspoonful of corn starch flour mixed thoroughly in six tablespoons of milk, one teaspoonful salt, mix this together; heat pan and have it hot, then beat the whites of the eggs, and stir quickly to the yolks, then pour into the pan, but do not stir it; when done it will be about an inch in thickness, fold it in halves when you put it on the plate. You can, for dessert, sprinkle sugar on and drop on currant jelly.

Omelette Soufflé.
MISS L. MIDDLETON.

One pt. boiled milk, three spoonfuls flour, yolks of seven eggs beaten with the flour. Season with pepper and salt. Add piece of butter size of an egg, mix well, then add the whites well beaten. Bake twenty minutes.

Salad Eggs.
MRS. SILLECK.

Boil ten eggs hard, take off shells, cut in halves, and place on dish garnished with whole lettuce leaves. Pour over the eggs Durkee's Salad Dressing and you will have a nice little dish for luncheon.

Omelette.

MRS. WALZ.

Four eggs, beat whites and yolks separately, half cup of milk, half (scant) teaspoon corn starch, fold in halves.

Omelette Soufflé.

FANNIE.

Take as many even tablespoonfuls sugar as you do eggs, beat the yolks, then stir in the sugar, add lemon juice or vanilla to flavor; when the whites are beaten to a froth, stir them in with the yolks. Heat in the oven the dish it is to be baked in; when all is ready grease the tin with butter, turn the mixture in and bake six or eight minutes.

Poached Eggs.

Have a skillet on the fire with boiling water, break the eggs, taking care that the yolks are not broken, pour them gently in the boiling water, three at a time, season with pepper and salt. Toast bread (after cutting the crust off) a delicate brown; when the eggs have simmered two minutes take up and place one on each slice of toast, a teaspoonful of vinegar added to water will prevent eggs from breaking.

Boiled Eggs.

The water must be *boiling* when the eggs are put in, to boil *soft* requires three minutes, hard five minutes.

To Test Eggs.

Place in a pan of water (cold), the fresher the egg is the sooner it will sink to the bottom.

Baked Omelette.

MRS. HULBURT.

Six eggs, one tablespoon of melted butter, little salt, and one gill of milk. Beat the whites and yolks of the eggs separately, mix all together and bake about fifteen minutes.

To Preserve Eggs.

The best method is to keep them in meal or bran; if necessary to keep them a long while. it is better to bury them in salt, which will preserve them in almost any climate.

VEGETABLES.

White Potatoes.

Wash clean, put in saucepan with just enough water to cover them, take about twenty minutes to cook, when done pour off water, throw in some salt, leave cover off and allow steam to evaporate, remove skins and serve, or mash, adding a little butter, pepper and salt, and milk, and smooth top nicely, add a few bits of butter, and place in oven to brown, or put in scollop shells, score with knife and brown.

Sweet Potatoes.

Same as *white*, or parboil them, peel, cut in halves, place in pudding dish, season with pepper and salt, plenty of butter, and a *very little* boiling water, brown nicely, and serve in same dish.

To Cook Potatoes under Meat.

Wash clean, peel, cut in halves (lengthwise), put in dripping-pan under meat, and season and baste same as meat.

Potato Chips.

Wash and peel some potatoes, cut ribbon-like, into long lengths, put them into cold water to remove strong potato flavor, drain them, and throw them into a pan with a little butter, and fry them a light brown. Take them out and place close to fire on a sieve to dry before serving, sprinkle a little salt over them.

Corn Chowder.

MRS. CHURCHMAN.

Six onions chopped fine, cook in a cup of butter until tender, then add six ears of corn cut from the cob, six potatoes peeled and sliced thin, six crackers, two qts. of water. Boil all together until potatoes are done, one qt. of milk boiled separately, add it last, and boil all together for a few moments. Do not stir while cooking, as it spoils the appearance of the dish. In winter use canned corn.

Corn and Tomato.

Corn boiled on the cob, then cut off and canned with tomatoes, in the usual manner of canning tomatoes, it will keep well and be an excellent dish. Have twice as much tomato as corn.

Potato Croquettes.

H. S. G.

Season cold mashed potatoes with pepper and salt. Beat to a cream with a tablespoonful of melted butter to every cupful of potato. Beat two or three eggs light, mix them in. Add some parsley chopped fine, roll into oval balls, dip in beaten egg, then in bread crumbs, fry in hot lard.

Cauliflowers.

Choose those that are close and white, take off the green leaves, look carefully that there are no caterpillars about stalk. Soak an hour in cold water, then boil in milk and water, skim several times. Take about twenty-five minutes to cook.

Green Peas.

Shell them and wash, boil twenty minutes in water just enough to cover them, season with pepper, salt and butter.

To Cook Egg Plant.
Miss Cripps.

Take the fruit fully ripe, cut in slices about a quarter of an inch thick and soak in cold salted water for two hours. Then dry the slices on a cloth, dip them in white of egg, and fry in boiling hot butter till nicely browned.

Escalloped Tomatoes.
Mrs. Hulbert.

Put a layer of tomatoes in an earthen dish, then one of bread or rolled cracker crumbs, with a little butter, pepper and salt, another of tomatoes, another of bread, till the dish is full. Bake three-quarters of an hour.

Asparagus.
Mrs. Silleck.

Scrape the stalks of two bundles of asparagus, wash in cold water and tie up again in bunches, place in pot with plenty of boiling water, a little salt and boil about twenty minutes. Then take out and drain it, cut off about two inches of the white part. Have ready toast laid on a dish, place asparagus tops on. Make nice fish sauce, only using the *water* in which the asparagus was boiled, instead of plain boiling water.

Spinach.

Pick spinach clean and wash in two or three waters. Place in saucepan with *very* little water, season with salt and pepper, when tender drain thoroughly in a sieve, chop fine, add a little butter, and garnish with hard-boiled eggs cut in slices.

Turnips.

Peel, cut in halves, boil until tender, then drain, mash and season with butter, pepper and salt.

Onions.

Peel and boil in water just enough to cover them, when nearly done throw off water, pour on one pt. of milk, a little butter, pepper and salt; when tender serve.

Macaroni.

MISS L. SILLECK.

Quantity of macaroni desired, break in small pieces, soak until tender on the range (put on in cold water). Place in pudding dish. Have ready grated cheese, milk and salt mixed together, pour on top of macaroni and set in oven to bake brown. Put bits of butter on top.

Saratoga Potatoes.

Peel and cut raw potatoes as thin a possible, fry in boiling lard until nearly done, take out for a few moments, then throw back into the hot lard and finish browning. This makes them swell. Season with salt.

String Beans.

String them, boil until tender, drain; add pepper, butter and salt and a little milk.

Stewed Tomatoes.

Place in a pan, pour boiling water over them, let stand until cool, when the skins will come off readily, after which put in saucepan, add butter, pepper and salt. Stew half-hour. Thicken with bread or cracker crumbs.

New England Baked Beans.

Mrs. Mason.

One pt. beans, small ones are best, soak over night, in the morning drain off the water and put in cold water to parboil, letting them stand about twenty minutes. On no account let them boil. Strain through a colander, and put in a deep brown earthen bean pot, allow half a lb. of fat pork put in the middle of the beans, one tablespoonful molasses, then cover with cold water, and bake seven hours, replenishing with cold water as it boils away.

Mushrooms.

Cut nice tender mushrooms in pieces, put in a saucepan and boil ten minutes, mix a little flour and butter together and stir in with mushrooms, add pepper and salt; boil once and serve.

Lima Beans.

Place in saucepan with water enough to cover them. When tender drain, season with pepper, salt, butter, and a very little milk, heated.

Green Corn.

Boil corn, *unhusked*, in salt water enough to cover (makes the corn more tender); when cooked remove husks and send to the table.

Succotash.

Take equal quantities of lima beans and corn cut from the cob, put in saucepan, cover with water, adding small piece of salt pork, cook half-hour, add small piece of butter, season with pepper and salt.

Stuffed Tomatoes.

Take nice large tomatoes; do not skin them, but scoop out a piece from the top of each, make a stuffing of bread crumbs, salt, pepper and raw egg; fill the tomatoes, heaping a little mound on each. About three-quarters of an hour to bake.

DRINKS.

Coffee, Tea, Chocolate and Cocoa.

It is much better to buy coffee whole, roast and grind it yourself; while hot stir in two eggs and a small piece of butter; put away in a tin canister for use.

Boiled Coffee.

Three tablespoonfuls of ground coffee to one pt. of *boiling* water; mix the coffee with cold water to a paste, add a well beaten egg to clear it; pour on boiling water; let it boil two minutes.

French Coffee.

Put the required quantity in a *French* coffee-pot, pour over *boiling* water, use the water at its first boil. Use Borden's condensed milk.

Tea.

Allow one teaspoonful of tea for each person; pour water on at its boiling point, let steep; never boil tea.

Chocolate.

Three heaping tablespoonfuls grated chocolate (Baker's plain), mix chocolate to a paste with cold water, then pour on one pt. of boiling water, boil twenty minutes; to this add one pt. of boiling milk, one tablespoonful whipped cream, sweetened to taste and flavor with vanilla, place on top of chocolate in each cup.

Cocoa.

Prepared nearly same as chocolate: directions on wrapper.

Choca.

New York Times.

Grate two ounces of chocolate, put it on the fire with a gill of water, stir it, when melted and rather thick add slowly half a pt. of boiling milk; do not allow it to boil after the milk is added; have ready one pt. of *cafe au lait*, made by mixing one teacupful of very strong coffee with one cupful boiling milk; now take the vessel containing the chocolate in one hand and the coffee in the other, and pour them slowly in a bowl from the 'height of about eighteen inches; add sugar, and serve instantly. Coffee renders the chocolate less heavy.

Breakfast and Side Dishes.

Fondee.
Mrs. Ludlow Thomas.

Two ozs. of butter, four ozs. bread crumbs, eight ozs. cheese, one cup sweet milk, three eggs. Cut the butter and cheese into small pieces and place them in a large bowl with the bread; on this pour scalding milk, after which add the yolks well beaten and also a little salt; mix well together, cover and place on the back of the range, stirring occasionally until all is dissolved, when add the whites of the eggs beaten to a stiff froth, place in a buttered dish and bake in a quick oven about twenty minutes. Serve the moment it is taken out. Many eat mustard on this.

Rice Waffles.
Miss Kumbell.

Take a large coffee cup of well boiled rice, stir in two eggs and a large tablespoonful corn starch, a teaspoonful salt, one qt. milk, a tablespoonful melted butter and self-raising flour enough to make a thick batter; if the flour is not self-raising put in a teaspoonful cream tartar and half teaspoon of soda; see that your waffle irons are well heated and greased.

Corn Oysters.
Mrs. Silleck.

One doz. ears of sweet corn grated, six eggs well beaten, two tablespoonfuls of flour, salt and pepper to taste, drop in boiling lard and fry brown; they should not be larger than an oyster when done.

Rice Croquettes.

Mrs. HULBERT.

One cup of rice boiled in one pt. of milk and one of water till tender, while boiling add butter size of an egg, two spoonfuls sugar, three eggs, juice and grated peel of one lemon, mix well. Make this into rolls about a finger long, and dip them first into the yolks of two eggs well beaten, then into cracker crumbs, and fry in hot lard.

Dainty Side Dish.

Mrs. BERGE.

Grate six parsnips, add one egg, one half teacup of flour, a little salt, dip up with a spoon and fry in a generous quantity of hot fat.

Hominy.

There are three sizes of hominy; large hominy (or samp) requires to be boiled from four to five hours over a gentle fire. It should be washed clean, and put in stew-pan with just enough water to cover it. It is eaten as a vegetable. Smaller hominy wash in two waters; then to one teacupful of hominy add one qt. of water and one teaspoonful salt and place the dish that contains it in a kettle of boiling water to prevent it from burning, else cook over a very gentle fire. Let it boil one hour, stirring it well with a spoon. It is generally eaten for breakfast. It is excellent sliced and fried after it has become cold.

Oatmeal.

One heaping cupful oatmeal, one qt. boiling water, one teaspoonful salt. Have the salted water boiling when you add the oatmeal, when mixed well do not stir more than is required to prevent it from burning to the bottom of the pot.

Oatmeal Porridge.
MRS. MERWIN.

Stir into a qt. and a pt. of boiling water or milk, half a lb. or one pt. of Heckers' oatmeal; add a little salt, and boil half an hour. Serve hot or cold, with milk, cream, syrup or sugar.

Breakfast Cakes.
MRS. MERWIN.

Take oatmeal porridge when cold, cut in slices, and dip into a batter made with eggs and flour, and brown. Serve with syrup or sugar.

German Toast.
MRS. WILCOX.

Take a loaf of bread, slightly stale, and after cutting off all the crust, cut it in pieces about three inches long, and one inch thick and wide. Soak these pieces for twenty minutes in a qt. of milk into which one egg has been beaten; then fry them in boiling lard, until they are a crisp brown. Serve with liquid wine sauce.

Boiled Rice.
NEW YORK TIMES.

Wash the rice well, put it on a quick fire with plenty of cold water, let it come to a boil, then pour off the water and add fresh cold water; do this a second time and then let it boil four or five minutes until the rice is tender, but not soft, then pour it into a colander and throw over it a qt. of cold water in which you have dissolved one teaspoonful of salt, drain thoroughly, set the colander over a saucepan of boiling water to steam uncovered for twenty or twenty-five minutes; never fails.

Maple Syrup for Hot Cakes.

One lb. of maple sugar, one lb. and a half of lump sugar, three qts. of water; break the maple sugar in small pieces, boil together five or ten minutes, skim and cool it; put away for use.

Oyster Macaroni.

NEW YORK TIMES.

Put one quarter lb. macaroni (broken in pieces) in salted boiling water; boil till quite tender, place a layer of macaroni in the bottom, then layer of oysters; repeat until the dish is full; pour over one halfcupful milk and juice, and put small pieces butter on top, and cover with bread crumbs and beaten egg. Baked in the oven and garnished with boiled eggs and parsley.

BREAD, ETC.

To Prepare Potatoes for Making into Bread.
MRS. HOYT.

Boil four or five potatoes of medium size in a qt. of water until they are thoroughly done. Drain off the water and add to it three tablespoonfuls of flour and beat them well together. Pass the potatoes through a colander and mix them well together with the flour and water. When sufficiently cool add a teacupful of yeast and stir down several times during the rising, and let it stand over night. Wet four qts. of flour with warm water and add to the above; when light mold down and let it rise again before making it into loaves.

Home-Made Yeast.
MRS. SILLECK.

Double handful of hops, tied in a thin lace bag, boiled in two qts. of water with eight large peeled potatoes, one penny's worth of bakers' yeast and one teaspoonful salt. When cold stir in two teacupfuls of wheat flour.

Bread.
MRS. THOMAS.

Put the quantity of flour you need in a pan, make a hole in the middle and pour in luke-warm water. Beat thoroughly with an iron spoon, add one-half or the whole of the potato yeast and let it stand to rise ; then knead well and let it stand to rise again. Make into loaves and let it rise in the pans. Bake in a quick oven one hour.

To Use Compressed Yeast.

Half cake of compressed yeast, dissolved in about half pt. of lukewarm water, make a hole in the flour and mix thoroughly; this quantity of yeast will make five small loaves.

Steamed Brown Bread.

Mrs. Greene.

Two cups Graham flour, two yellow corn meal, two of rye *meal* (not flour), four cups of water and one of molasses; two teaspoonfuls soda; steam four hours. By adding raisins and making a nice sauce, it makes a very nice and simple pudding that one need not be afraid to have children eat heartily of.

Graham Bread.

Mrs. Ruland.

Six teacups of Graham flour, one teacup wheat flour, one teacup molasses, one teacup yeast; stir to a thin batter and leave to rise over night; when light add salt and a little Graham flour to thicken, leaving it to rise again, not putting the hands in until molding. This makes one loaf.

Parker House Rolls.

Mrs. J. Parker.

One pt. new milk (scald it). Put in a pan one qt. of flour, one tablespoonful of sugar, two of melted lard, half cup of yeast; cool the milk sufficiently, then mix all together. Let it rise, then add one qt. of flour, stir all together, add a little soda, let them rise again, then roll, cut and turn in roll shape, put in pans to rise again; when raised bake in a quick oven ten minutes.

Boiled Indian Bread.

Mrs. Packer.

Four teacups Indian meal, two of wheat flour, three and a half of sour milk, two teaspoonfuls soda, two of salt. Boil in a well greased farina boiler eight hours; after boiling four hours turn the bread out on a plate, and put the top of the loaf in the bottom of the boiler.

Corn Bread.

Mrs. Swalm.

One and a half cups of Indian meal, one egg, two tablespoonfuls flour, two tablespoonfuls molasses, one tablespoonful cream tartar, half tablespoonful soda, the least bit of butter or lard. Bake in quick oven.

Corn Bread.

Mrs. Smith.

Two cups Indian meal, one of flour, two eggs, one pt. of sweet milk, two teaspoonfuls cream tartar, one of soda, two tablespoonfuls sugar, one large tablespoonful butter; make it so it will pour in pan. Bake in quick oven.

Raised Biscuit.

Mrs. Packer.

Two qts. flour, half teacup of butter, same of lard rubbed into the flour, two tablespoonfuls of yeast, one pt. warm milk, a little salt. Mix all together with as little kneading as possible; when light roll and cut out with very little flour on the board; let stand in the pan about an hour and bake in quick oven.

Muffins.

MRS. CONE.

One tablespoonful sugar, two of butter, one cup milk, half cup water, three cups flour, two and a half teaspoonfuls baking powder. Hot roll pans and hot oven.

Steamed Graham Bread.

MRS. RULAND.

Three cups Graham flour, two cups Indian meal (yellow), two cups sour milk, one cup molasses, two teaspoonfuls soda, one teaspoonful salt. Mix the milk, molasses and soda together, then add the meal and flour; mix all the ingredients thoroughly. Steam four hours in a mold.

Breakfast Rolls.

MRS. PACKER.

Rub one oz. of butter in a qt. of flour, one egg well beaten, two tablespoons of yeast, a little salt, one pint of milk, mix together in a soft dough. Roll out in the morning without adding any flour, let stand about half an hour to rise, then bake in a quick oven.

Corn Muffins.

S. C.

Two cups of yellow corn meal, one cup cold boiled rice, one egg, one tablespoonful lard, two cups milk, a little salt, two teaspoonfuls cream tartar, one of soda. Rub the lard well in the dry meal, then the rice, then the milk, egg well beaten, salt and soda and cream tartar. Bake in cup pans from half to three-quarters of an hour.

Third Bread Muffins.
Mrs. Wilder.

One cup Indian meal, two of rye meal, three of flour, one pt. milk or water, half cup of yeast, same of molasses. Just before baking add one teaspoonful soda, must be well raised to be good.

Rice Pancakes.
Mrs. Hobart.

One qt. of milk, five eggs, thicken with half rice flour and half wheat, about three teaspoonfuls yeast powder; do not add the powder until just before baking.

Muffins.
Mrs. Packer.

One qt. milk, two qts. flour, three eggs, half teacup yeast, half teaspoon salt; when raised add half teaspoon soda just before baking. Bake in muffin rings in quick oven.

Corn Balls.
Mrs. Churchman.

One qt. Indian meal well scalded, one egg, teaspoonful salt, tablespoonful molasses. Fry in *very hot lard*.

Wheat Puffs.
Mrs. Churchman.

Stir together a pt. of cold milk and a pt. and a quarter of flour, teaspoonful of salt. Take gem pans, heat them very hot on the top of the stove, put a small piece of butter in each pan, and while it is sizzling pour in the batter. Bake twenty minutes; the last ten minutes set the pan on the top of the grating of the oven.

Breakfast Cakes.
MRS. AVILA.

One cup of Graham flour, one cup of wheat flour (or two cups of wheat and no Graham), one pt. milk, one egg and little salt. Stir the egg when beaten into the milk, then into the flour, after it is well beaten together bake in a hot oven in *hot* gem pans.

Light Tea Biscuit.

One qt. sifted flour, add two teaspoonfuls Royal Baking Powder and one tablespoonful butter, mix with one pt. of milk or water, with one half teaspoon salt dissolved in it; roll out one half-inch thick, cut with plain cutter, set on buttered pans close together, bake in hot oven.

Johnny Cake.
MRS. TITUS.

One qt. sour milk, two tablespoonfuls sugar and piece of butter size of an egg, two teaspoons soda. Made about as thick as pound cake.

Crumpets.
MRS. J. MOORE.

One pt. sweet milk, one tablespoon of yeast, a very little sugar, small piece of butter, make them quite thick, let them stand over night; in the morning add two eggs. Bake in rings on a griddle, turn when done on one side.

Indian Cake.
MRS. ALLEN.

Half cup of Indian meal, one cup flour, half cup sugar, one cup milk, one egg, salt, one teaspoonful of soda.

Vienna Pocket-Books.

Have ready in a bowl a tablespoonful of butter, warm it a little to make it soft, stir around with spoon. One qt. unsifted flour, add two heaping teaspoonfuls Royal Baking Powder, mix and sift thoroughly together, place in a bowl with the butter, milk enough to form a dough of usual stiffness according to the flour (about three-quarters of a pt.), half teaspoon of salt, put into milk, then stir in flour with a spoon, form into dough, turn out on board, knead sufficiently to make smooth. Roll out half an inch thick and cut with a large round cutter. Fold over in shape of a pocket-book, wetting a little between the folds to make them keep together. Place on buttered pans, do not allow them to touch, wash the top of each with milk. Bake immediately in hot oven twenty minutes.

Queen Muffins.

Mrs. J. Hebert.

One qt. milk, three-fourths of a cup of yeast, two tablespoonfuls white sugar, one tablespoonful of lard or butter, one teaspoonful salt, flour to make a good batter, two eggs; let the batter (leaving out the eggs) rise over night. In the morning beat the eggs very light, stir into the batter and bake in muffin rings twenty minutes in a *quick oven.*

Soda Biscuit.

Mrs. Thomas.

Three pts. of flour, one pt. milk, one half cup butter rubbed into the flour, with salt and two teaspoonfuls cream tartar, one of soda, dissolved in the milk. Corn meal can be made in the same manner, by taking half the quantity of flour and the rest of the corn meal.

Indian Pone.

MRS. THOMAS.

One qt. of corn meal, piece of butter size of an egg, scalded with one qt. of boiling milk. When cold add four eggs beaten very light, salt, two tablespoonfuls of brewers' yeast. Let it stand until light, then bake.

Soda Biscuit.

MRS. SILLECK.

One qt. of flour, one tablespoonful butter, same of lard, teaspoonful salt, two teaspoonfuls Royal Baking Powder and one pt. of milk; cut in finger-lengths and about two inches thick.

Rice Muffins.

MRS. HEBERT.

One cup boiled rice, one pt. flour, two eggs, one qt. milk, or enough to make a thin batter, one tablespoonful lard or butter, one teaspoonful salt. Beat hard and bake quickly.

Pop Overs.

MRS. J. MOORE.

Two cups milk, two cups flour, two eggs, a small piece of butter melted and put in the last thing, a little salt. Fill the cups half full and bake in a quick oven. Use earthenware cups.

Rice Cakes.

MRS. WILDER.

Half pt. rice boiled and mashed smooth, add one cup of milk, three eggs beaten separately and flour to make a stiff batter, one spoonful sugar, salt. Bake in rings or gem pans.

Rye Pan Cakes.

MRS. ROBBINS.

One pt. milk, one qt. fine rye flour, two cups wheat flour, one cup sugar, two eggs, two large spoonfuls of molasses, one teaspoonful of salt, same of soda. Drop from a spoon into hot lard.

Rusk.

MRS. TITUS.

Take one cup of unbaked bread, when light thoroughly mix in half cup of butter and half cup of sugar and a little soda. Make out and bake when very light.

Rye Cakes.

MRS. WILDER.

Two cups of milk, half cup of sugar, one egg, one teaspoonful soda, two of cream tartar. Rye or Graham flour, make a stiff batter to drop, not roll out, bake in gem pans.

Oatmeal Cakes.

MISS L. PARKER.

Two cups of oatmeal, mixed with a pint of sour milk (or sweet), one cup of flour, a little salt and one egg. Bake like any griddle cakes.

Currant Buns.

MRS. PALMER.

Mix together half cup of butter with one cup of sugar, stir in half cup of milk and half cup of yeast, after stirring very thick with flour set to rise over night. In the morning mix in two eggs and one cup of currants, with a little lemon essence or other flavoring. Work stiff enough with flour to mold into buns. When very light bake in a hot oven, and when done wash over the top a little white of egg and molasses.

Graham Puffs, Mohican House, Lake George.
Miss Sweet.

One pt. sour milk, one egg, one teaspoonful saleratus, one teaspoonful sugar. Quite a thick batter.

Waffles.
Mrs. Thomas.

One qt. of milk, three eggs, two-thirds of a cup of lard, a pinch of salt, some brewers' yeast, flour to make as thick as flannel cakes. Simmer the milk, then take it off the fire and add the shortening, let it stand till cool, then pour into the flour, beating it all the time. Add the eggs and beat again; lastly the yeast and let rise about four hours.

Bran Muffins.
Mrs. Thomas.

Two cups of sour milk, one cup of sweet milk, three eggs, two-thirds of a cup of sugar, one large teaspoonful soda, a lump of butter size of a walnut, melt it, bran flour to make it thick enough to drop off the spoon. Bake in muffin rings.

French Rolls.
Mrs. Ide.

One qt. of flour, one pt. of yeast, half pt. of milk, one cup of butter and lard, one teaspoonful sugar, a little salt, set to sponge, when light make into a loaf (not stiff), when very light roll out and cut into cakes. Spread with melted butter and make like turn-overs. Bake ten minutes in a hot oven.

Rye Drop Cakes.
Mrs. Kendall.

Two cups rye meal, one egg, one cup yellow Indian meal, one tablespoonful molasses, one teaspoonful cream tartar, half teaspoonful soda. Mix to the consistency of pound cake, and drop a tablespoonful of the mixture in boiling lard. Fry brown.

Puffs.

MISS THURSTON.

One pt. of new milk, six eggs, half cup butter. Boil the milk, leaving out a little with which to wet the flour, make a thin batter as for starch. Mix this with the milk, while it boils. Then add flour, dry, stirring it all the time, until the paste is thick enough for a spoon to stand up in while boiling. Be careful to have the paste thick, and not burn in the cooking. Add the butter, stirring it in; when cool add the eggs *one at a time*, beating each well in until the six are mixed in. It should then be of the color and consistency of pound cake. If it is not add flour until thick enough. Drop a small tablespoonful into boiling lard as you would doughnuts, cooking them twice as long. Take the puffs out with a skimmer and while hot sprinkle freely with cinnamon and sugar.

Straws.

MRS. SILLECK.

One qt. Heckers' prepared flour, add one pt. of milk, one tablespoonful butter, one egg, roll out as for biscuit, cut in diamond shape, fry in boiling lard. Eat with butter same as biscuit.

Squash Biscuit.

MRS. HAXTUN.

One small bowl of marrow squash cooked, one teacup white sugar, three tablespoonfuls of melted butter, three of yeast, three of milk, a little salt, and as much flour as can be stirred in with a spoon (until it comes off dry from the sides of the bowl). Mix all at night, and in the morning dissolve a small teaspoonful of saleratus and put it through the biscuit with your fingers, then roll, cut in biscuit and bake, they need a pretty hot fire. Add no more flour in the morning except what is necessary to roll out.

Buckwheat Cakes.

MRS. MASON.

One qt. buckwheat flour, half a cup of yeast, one tablespoonful salt, warm water enough to make a batter not very thick, beat it well with a large spoon, and set it to rise about eight hours, heat the griddle, and rub it hard with a coarse cloth, have a piece of pork about four inches square on a fork, rub the griddle with it, and turn the batter on in small cakes while hot.

Soft Waffles.

P.

Three pts. of milk, one coffee cup of yeast, same of butter (scant), eight eggs, a little salt, not very stiff with flour, like a thin batter.

Puffet.

I.

One qt. of milk, two tablespoonfuls brewers' yeast, same of sugar, one of butter. As much flour as you can stir in with a spoon.

Farina Griddle Cakes.

MRS. MERWIN.

Cook the farina as directed for ice pudding; dilute with milk to the consistency of a batter, add two eggs well beaten, salt to taste. Bake on a hot griddle.

Marion Harland, in her "Breakfast, Luncheon and Tea," says of Heckers' self-raising flour: "Heckers' flour I have found invaluable in cake making. Indeed, I have never achieved any thing short of triumphant success when I have used it."

PUDDINGS AND SAUCES.

Suet Pudding.
Miss B. Johnes.

One cup of raisins, one cup currants, one cup suet chopped fine, one cup milk or water, one cup bread crumbs soaked, two apples chopped fine, one cup molasses, two eggs, two teaspoonfuls cloves, two teaspoonfuls cinnamon, one of allspice, two of soda, four cups sifted flour. Boil three hours.

Delmonico Pudding.
Mrs. Parrott, Keokuk.

One qt. of milk, three tablespoonfuls corn starch mixed with a little of the milk, put into the qt. of milk just before it boils; boil three minutes, then stir in the yolks of five eggs beaten with six tablespoons of sugar; flavor with lemon or vanilla. Place in pudding dish, spread on top the beaten whites of the five eggs, put into the oven until it is a delicate brown. Eaten cold with sweetened cream.

Chocolate Pudding.
Mrs. Sumner.

One qt. of milk, two cups sugar, six tablespoonfuls of corn starch, the yolks of three eggs, quarter lb. of chocolate, one tablespoonful of vanilla and a little salt; mix all the ingredients together with a little of the cold milk, scald the rest and pour into it the mixture, stirring constantly till it thickens. Use a farina kettle. Make a merangue of the whites of the eggs for the top.

Indian Pudding.

MRS. SUMNER.

Boil one qt. of milk, stir seven tablespoonfuls of corn meal into nearly one cup of molasses, pour the boiling milk over it, stir thoroughly, add a little salt and one pt. of cold milk. Bake in a moderate oven four hours, the last hour with decreasing heat.

Baked Blackberry Pudding.

MISS F. SILLECK.

One qt. of milk, three eggs, half lb. of suet chopped fine, *Heckers' prepared* flour, enough to make a stiff batter, add two qts. of berries (flour to prevent sinking). Bake one hour in a moderate oven.

Cottage Pudding.

MRS. WALZ.

With two cups of flour mix two teaspoonfuls baking powder, one egg, one tablespoonful of butter, three-quarters of a cup of sugar, half cup of milk; flavor to taste. Bake quickly. To be eaten with liquid sauce.

Batter Pudding.

MRS. REYNOLDS.

One pt. of milk, four eggs beaten separately, two cups of flour, one teaspoonful salt, one pinch of soda. Bake three-quarters of an hour. (Pinch must mean very little).

Tapioca Pudding.

MRS. QUIRK.

One cup of tapioca dissolved in cold water, six eggs, two qts. of milk, sweeten to taste, nutmeg and a little wine.

Randall Pudding.

MISS ADA JENNISON.

Quarter lb. of carrots, same of potatoes, grated raw, same of suet and flour, half lb. currants, some citron, a little nutmeg and some cinnamon. Boil three hours, serve with wine sauce.

Back-About Pudding.

MRS. WILDER.

To one tumbler tapioca add one tumbler cold water, soak over night, in the morning add three more tumblers cold water, set on the range, stir, when transparent stir in one tumbler sugar and one tumbler currant jelly until dissolved; turn into jelly mold. To be eaten cold with cream and sugar.

English Plum Pudding.

MRS. MAJOR.

One bowl raisins, same of currants, same of suet, one and a half bowls bakers' bread crumbs, half lb. citron, one teaspoonful cinnamon, same of allspice, ten eggs, one cup of brandy; make into two puddings, boil five hours, be sure to keep covered with water and keep boiling. Eat with wine sauce.

Chocolate Pudding.

MRS. SWALM.

Boil one qt. of milk with one oz. of grated chocolate, sweeten and flavor with vanilla or lemon. When thoroughly boiled let it cool fifteen minutes, then stir in the yolks of six eggs well beaten. Bake in a pudding dish until it hardens like custard. Have the whites of the eggs beaten to a stiff froth, stir into it six tablespoonfuls of pulverized sugar, spread over the top of the pudding, and brown in the oven. It should be eaten perfectly cold.

German Puffs.

Mrs. Smith.

Two cups flour, two cups milk, two eggs, salt. Bake in cups, quick oven. This quantity will make ten puffs.

Boiled Pudding.

Mrs. Swalm.

One cup molasses, same of chopped suet, same of chopped raisins, one and a half cups currants, same of milk, one teaspoonful soda in the milk, one teaspoonful salt, flour to make it the thickness of cake. Put in pudding boiler and boil steadily three hours. Sauce made of butter and sugar to eat on it.

Brown Betty.

Mrs. Parrott, Keokuk.

Put a layer of tart apples into a pudding-dish, sprinkle a little sugar and cinnamon over the apples, then add a layer of bread-crumbs and some little pieces of butter, proceed with layers of apple and bread-crumbs until the dish is full, then set in oven and bake about one hour. To be eaten with boiled sauce or cream; if the latter, it is nice cold.

Apple Slump.

Mrs. Cone.

Two qts. of apples, one pt. molasses, one tablespoonful cinnamon, same of butter. Make a crust same as for short biscuit, line the sides only of a porcelain pot with the crust about half an inch thick, quarter the apples without peeling and place them in the pot, and pour the molasses over them with the cinnamon and butter. Cover with top-crust and let it simmer three hours on the back of the range. One half hour before serving place in the oven and let brown.

Graham Pudding.
Mrs. Cone.

One half coffee cup Graham flour, half cup molasses, quarter of a cup melted butter, half a cup of sweet milk, one egg, one even teaspoon soda, salt, half cup raisins, same of currants, one teaspoon cloves, half a teaspoon cinnamon, quarter of a nutmeg. Steam two and a half hours.

English Plum Pudding.
Mrs. Silleck.

One loaf of bakers' bread soaked in milk, one lb. of chopped suet, five eggs, half teaspoon of cloves, two teaspoonfuls mace, three of cinnamon, one small cup of molasses, one teaspoonful baking powder dissolved in molasses, little salt, one and a half lbs. of raisins, one lb. currants, half lb. citron (roll fruit in a little of the flour). Place in pudding form and boil four hours. Will keep three months.

Sponge Pudding.
Mrs. Swalm.

Take four eggs and weigh them, take their weight in butter, flour and sugar, mix the butter and sugar to a light froth, add the eggs and flour. Boil two hours in a pudding-boiler. Beat sugar and butter to a light froth, to that add warm milk, and you have a sauce to eat on the pudding when served. Must be eaten warm.

Fried Bread, or "Le Pain-Perdu."
Mrs. Churchman.

Sliced bakers' bread dipped in heated, and one or two eggs beaten, fry in hot lard. Before serving pour over this sauce: Yolk of one egg, one cup of sugar, one tablespoonful butter, when mixed pour in three quarters of a cup of boiling water, beat the white of the egg and stir in a very little pinch of cinnamon.

Kiss Pudding.

Miss L. Middleton.

One qt. milk, three tablespoonfuls corn starch, yolks of four eggs, half cup sugar, a little salt. Put part of the milk, salt and sugar on the stove and let it boil. Dissolve the corn starch in the rest and stir into the milk; while it is boiling add the yolks and then flour to suit, flavor with vanilla. Frosting flavored with lemon spread on the top, then put in the oven to brown, saving a little to put on top after having taken it from the oven, and put cocoanut on the whole.

Orange Pudding.

Mrs. L. Smith.

Take four good-sized oranges, peel, seed and cut into small pieces, add a cup of sugar and let it stand. Into one qt. of nearly boiling milk stir two tablespoonfuls of corn starch mixed with a little water and the yolks of three eggs, when done let it cool and then mix with the oranges. Make a frosting of the whites of the eggs and half a cup of powdered sugar, spread over the pudding and set in the oven to brown. It is excellent.

Cracker Pudding.

Mrs. Packer.

One qt. milk, four eggs well beaten, four tablespoonfuls rolled cracker, two tablespoonfuls melted butter. Bake one hour.

Batter Pudding.

Mrs. Packer.

Twelve tablespoonfuls flour, nine eggs, one teaspoon salt, one qt. milk. Beat the yolks of the eggs thoroughly, stir in the flour and add the milk slowly. Beat the whites of the eggs to a stiff froth and add just before putting in the oven. Bake an hour.

Whitpot.

Mrs. Cone.

Scald one qt. milk, take the yolks of four eggs and three tablespoonfuls of Indian meal and four tablespoonfuls molasses, spoonful salt, beat all together. When thoroughly beaten pour in the boiling milk and then boil twenty minutes. Serve hot, and just before serving grate in a little nutmeg.

Whortleberry Pudding.

Mrs. Packer.

One pt. flour, one and a half pts. of whortleberries stirred carefully in the flour, half teaspoon salt, one teaspoon soda, sifted in dry, one teacup molasses. Mix all carefully together so as not to break the berries, and boil in a tin pudding-boiler two hours.

Boiled Suet Pudding.

Mrs. Packer.

One lb. bread crumbs, one lb. sugar, six ozs. suet chopped fine, rind and juice of two lemons, three eggs, one cup milk, half lb. raisins, half lb. currants. Boil three hours in tin pudding-boiler.

Orange Fritters.

Mrs. F. Taylor.

Quarter lb. of flour, one large or two small eggs, two oranges cut in about five slices each. Put the yolks of the eggs in the flour and mix, adding half cup milk (or more if needed), beat into a batter, and add half spoonful salt, one teaspoonful melted butter. Beat the whites of the eggs to a froth and add to the batter just as you are going to fry, mix slowly. Drop the oranges into the batter and fry in hot lard. Serve on a napkin with powdered sugar.

Creme Frite.

Mrs. F. Taylor.

Three eggs to a quarter lb. of sugar and quarter lb. flour. Mix them thoroughly, add half pt. milk; put it upon the fire and boil five minutes, stirring it all the time; flavor with a teaspoonful of vanilla. Grease a platter with melted butter, pour your cooked batter upon it, and smooth it flat, and put it away to cool. When it is firm, cut in any shape you please, and roll it in bread or cracker crumbs and egg, and fry in hot lard.

Peach or Apple Fritters.

Mrs. Maxwell.

One qt. flour, two teaspoonfuls yeast powder rubbed dry through the flour, a little salt, one egg, water enough to make a stiff batter, peaches or apples sliced very thin, fry in very hot lard and plenty of it, as the more lard and hotter it is, the the lighter and drier will be the fritters.

Webster Pudding.

Miss L. Middleton.

One cup molasses, one cup milk, one cup of suet, half cup brandy or wine, if you like, one teaspoon saleratus, one teaspoon cloves, one teaspoonful cinnamon, one half nutmeg, two cups of currants, one teaspoonful salt. Mix as soft as pound cake and steam two hours; serve with wine sauce.

Evening Post Pudding.

Miss B. Johnes.

One pt. grated bread crumbs, one qt. milk, two tablespoonfuls sugar, yolks of four eggs, butter size of an egg, grated lemon rind. Top after baking; four whites beaten with four tablespoonfuls powdered sugar, juice of a lemon. Put jelly (any kind) between the pudding and meringue.

Cocoanut Pudding.

Mrs. Valentine.

One grated cocoanut, one pt. milk, three eggs. Sweeten to taste. Bake slowly.

Puff Pudding.

Mrs. Middleton.

One tablespoon of flour, one egg, one tablespoon of milk, one teaspoon melted butter.

Green Corn Pudding.

Mrs. Middleton.

Twelve ears of green corn, grate it, one qt. sweet milk, quarter lb. of fresh butter, four eggs well beaten, pepper and salt to taste, stir well together, bake in a buttered dish. By adding quarter lb. of sugar, and eating with sauce makes a nice dessert.

Apple or Fruit Pudding.

M. L. T.

Beat to a cream a lump of butter size of an egg, with a cup of sugar, the yolks of three eggs, two slices of bread previously soaked in milk, then add two apples finely sliced, a little lemon rind, when mixed stir in the whites of the eggs lightly. Boil in a mold for one hour steady, serve with wine or hard sauce, cherries or blackberries may be used instead of apples.

Scotch Pudding.

Mrs. Roberts.

One cup of cream, same of milk, one egg, one teaspoonful saleratus, a little salt, and flour enough to make a stiff batter. Fill a pudding dish about two-thirds full of sliced apples (first butter the dish), pour the batter over the apples and bake one hour.

Poor Man's Pudding.

MRS. CORWIN.

One cup suet chopped fine, same of raisins chopped, one cup molasses, same of milk, three cups wheat flour, one teaspoonful soda. Boil in pudding mold one and a half hours.

Neapolitan Pudding.

MRS. J. HEBERT.

One large cup fine bread crumbs soaked in milk, three-quarters cup of sugar, one lemon, juice and grated rind, six eggs, half lb. stale sponge cake, half lb. almond macaroons, half cup of jelly or jam, and one small tumbler of sherry wine, half cup of milk poured upon the bread crumbs, one tablespoonful melted butter. Rub the butter and sugar together, put the beaten yolks in next, then the soaked bread crumbs, the lemon juice and rind, and beat to a smooth light paste before adding the whites. Butter your mold very well and put in the bottom a light layer of dry crumbs; upon this one of macaroons laid evenly and closely together. Wet these with wine and cover with a layer of the mixture, then with slices of sponge cake spread thickly with jelly or jam, next macaroons wet with wine, more custard, sponge cake and jam and so on until the mold is full, putting a layer of the mixture on top; cover closely and steam in an oven three-quarters of an hour, then remove the cover to brown the top. Turn out carefully into a dish and pour over it a sauce made of currant jelly warmed and beaten up with two tablespoonfuls melted butter and a glass of pale sherry.

Cabinet Pudding.

MRS. MASON.

Make a sheet of cake, cut in halves; cut up peaches and lay between and on top. Serve with sweet sauce.

Queen of Puddings.
Mrs. C. Ide.

One qt. of new cold milk poured over one pt. of bread crumbs. Beat a piece of butter the size of an egg and a cup of sugar to a cream; add the yolks of eggs, flour and grated rind of a lemon. Beat this up with the bread and milk and bake forty minutes. When done put aside to cool, and when cool spread over it fresh fruit or any kind of preserves. (It is delicious made with strawberries, but makes a very nice pudding even if the fruit be omitted altogether.) Beat the whites of the eggs, adding three tablespoonfuls of fine sugar and juice of lemon, spread over the whole and brown slightly in oven. To be served cold.

Bread Pudding.
Miss Kumbel.

One pt. bread crumbs, one qt. milk, yolks of four eggs, one cup sugar, one tablespoonful butter, grated rind of one lemon, let it cool. Meringue—beat up the whites, one cup of sugar, the juice of the lemon, spread over the pudding, put in the oven a few minutes, and make a wine sauce if you choose for it.

Cider Pudding.
Mrs. Baker.

One pt. of cider, one cup molasses, same of chopped suet, four cups sifted flour, one teaspoonful salt, same of soda, raisins and currants. Boil three hours.

Carrot Pudding.
Mrs. Haxtun.

Quarter lb. of suet chopped fine, same of flour, same of grated carrot, same of grated raw potatoes, same of currants, one cup of molasses, salt. Boil it three hours and a half.

Dandy Pudding.

MISS KUMBEL.

One qt. milk, four eggs, four tablespoonfuls sugar, one tablespoonful flour or corn starch; beat yolks, sugar and flour together. Boil milk and throw on the custard, put on the fire, stirring constantly until thick as soft custard, then put into dish. Beat the whites to a froth with four tablespoonfuls sugar, flavor with vanilla, put on custard and place in the oven a few minutes. Makes eight cups when baked.

Quaking Pudding.

MRS. MASON.

Scald one qt. cream, when almost cold add to it four eggs well beaten, one and a half spoonfuls of flour, some nutmeg and sugar, tie it close in a buttered cloth, boil it one hour and turn it out with care lest it break. Sauce—melted butter, wine and sugar.

Fig Pudding.

MRS. HAXTUN.

Half lb. of figs, same of flour, two eggs, half lb. suet, a little sugar, a little wine. Boil in a tin form four hours.

Lemon Pudding.

MISS CARRIE.

Take two large lemons, one lb. of loaf sugar, one pt. of cream or one pt. of milk, with three ozs. of butter, nine eggs, two tablespoonfuls of flour, grate the yellow rind of one lemon, the juice of both, mix the butter and sugar thoroughly together, beat the eggs well and add them, then the cream and flour, add the juice of the lemons the last thing. Line the dish with a rich paste, bake three-quarters of an hour in a moderate oven.

Ice Pudding.
Mrs. Merwin.

Boil in farina boiler three pts. of milk or one qt. of water: while boiling sprinkle in slowly one quarter of a lb., or four large tablespoonfuls of farina; continue a brisk boiling for about half an hour, when done turn into jelly molds, and place it in ice or in cold water to stiffen. It thus becomes a beautiful ornament for the table, and may be eaten with wine or other sauce, pulverized sugar or any condiment more pleasing to the taste. This pudding, even when a day or so old, may be sliced and fried brown, and forming an excellent dish for breakfast.

Rice Pudding without Eggs.

Six large tablespoonfuls rice well washed, to one qt. of milk, five tablespoonfuls sugar, quarter of a lb. of raisins, stoned; flavor with vanilla.

Sauces for Puddings.
S. B. D.

White of one egg beaten very stiff, then sweeten and flavor with wine.

Wine Sauce.

Half cup of butter, one cup of sherry wine, two cups sugar. Beat the butter and sugar to a cream, add a little water, let it come to a boil, take it off the fire and add the wine.

Pudding Sauce.
Mrs. Quirk.

One cup of white sugar, one cup butter, one egg, one wine glass of wine or brandy, one nutmeg. When all is well *beaten* add two tablespoonfuls *boiling* water. Then beat it well and it is ready for use.

Spice Sauce.

Boil three-quarters of a pt. of water, one cupful of sugar, twenty minutes, remove from the fire and add one teaspoonful each extract of mace, cloves and ginger.

Mock Cream Sauce.

Miss M. Moore.

One qt. of milk boiled, one cup sugar, two eggs, one teaspoonful vanilla, same of corn starch, stir together and put in the milk when it boils.

Lemon Sauce.

Miss M. Moore.

One large cup sugar, nearly half cup butter, one egg, one lemon, all the juice, half the rind grated, one teaspoonful nutmeg, three tablespoonfuls boiling water; cream the butter and sugar, beat in the egg and nutmeg, beat hard ten minutes, and add a spoonful at a time the boiling water, put in a tin pail and set within the uncovered top of the tea kettle, which you must keep boiling until the steam heats the sauce very hot, but not to boiling; stir constantly.

Farina Jelly Sauce.

Mrs. Merwin.

Beat one fresh egg fine, and mix it with two qts. of good milk; add half a lb. of granulated or other white sugar, one teaspoonful of extract of bitter almond, and one teaspoonful extract of vanilla, and one tablespoonful alcohol; stir all together and it is fit for immediate use. The alcohol may be omitted and any other spirit subtituted, or two teaspoonfuls of either kind of flavoring, or other flavoring may be used as taste or fancy may prefer. Alcohol prevents rapid souring in warm weather.

Another.

Mrs. Avila.

One cup sugar, one egg beaten to a stiff froth, one small cup water. Stir in a teaspoonful flour, let it come to a boil, then drop in a piece of butter the size of a walnut. Let it stand until about milk warm, then pour into the egg and sugar. Flavor as you please.

Having used Borden's Condensed Milk in puddings and sauces over *twenty years*, I take much pleasure in recommending it. Mrs. I. U. Silleck.

PASTRY, PIES, ETC.

Pie Crust.
Mrs. Valentine.

Four heaping cups flour, good half cup of lard, one full cup of ice water, a little salt. Rub the shortening in the flour, then add ice water and salt.

Another.
Mrs. Walz.

One qt. plain flour, two cups shortening, half lard and half butter, little salt, one cup ice water. Rub the shortening through the flour dry before wetting it.

Puff Paste.
Mrs. Thomas.

One and a quarter lbs. of flour, one lb. of washed butter, weigh half a lb. of flour out to roll in. Cut your butter into four pieces, cut one quarter very fine and mix it with the remainder of your flour with half a pt. of *very cold* water. Roll it out and put in one-quarter of the butter and a little flour, roll again and so on till it is done. Secret of puff paste is keeping it very cold.

Eastern Shore Potato Pie.
Cousin Vinnie.

Three lbs. of prepared sweet potato, six eggs, half pt. of milk, two cups sugar, half lb. of butter, two tablespoonfuls essence of lemon. Bake in bottom crust only.

Mince Meat for Pies.
Mrs. Cone.

One lb. raw meat chopped very fine, half lb. suet, one lb. apples, half lb. raisins, same of currants, quarter lb. of citron, one teaspoonful of cinnamon, same of cloves, same of nutmeg, same of allspice, one lb. sugar, half cup of molasses, one tablespoonful salt, one gill brandy, cider enough to moisten. Chop all together excepting the meat, add that last.

Mince Pies.
Mrs. Valentine.

Three gals. cider, three lbs. currants, one lb. citron, one lb. orange peel, six lb. raisins, cloves, cinnamon and nutmeg to taste, one lb. suet, twelve lbs. meat, nearly as much more of apples. Boil all together and put it in a stone jar, sprinkle brown sugar over it, sweeten to taste. Add brandy when you make the pies.

Cream Pie.
Miss Ada Maxwell.

Make a good pie crust, line the pie pans and bake. The cream—one pt. milk, half cup flour, yolks of two eggs, juice and grated rind of a large lemon, salt and sugar to taste, prepare as for corn starch, smooth the flour with a little of the cold milk, take the remainder of the milk, add the sugar and salt, place it over the fire and when nearly boiling stir in the flour and stir continually until it thickens, then pour it over the yolks of the eggs, which have been previously well beaten, flavor with the lemon, and pour the mixture on to the pie crust, be sure that it is thoroughly cooked so as not to have a raw taste. Beat the the whites of the eggs to a very stiff froth, add a tablespoonful powdered sugar and a little lemon juice; spread it over the pie with a knife, then set it in a *very very* hot oven for a minute and let it become a delicate brown. The oven must be very hot else it will make it tough.

Cocoanut Pies.
MRS. VALENTINE.

One qt. milk, four eggs, one large cocoanut, a spoonful of flour.

Cream Pie.
MRS. ROBERTS.

One pt. of milk, half cup sugar, one heaping tablespoonful corn starch, yolks of two eggs, a little salt. Mix the corn starch with a little cold milk, adding the sugar, egg and salt; boil the rest of the milk and stir in the igredients while boiling. Have a single crust baked ready for the cream. For frosting beat the whites of two eggs, after beating add two tablespoonfuls powdered sugar, spread it on the pie and brown it in the oven.

Apple Pie.
MRS. CONE.

Peel and slice apples in a baking plate, cover with a rich crust, add a very little water, place in the oven and bake until apples are done. Then remove the crust and turn over on a clean plate; mash the apples and season with sugar, butter and cinnamon and place on the crust again.

Lemon Cheesecakes.
MRS. L. THOMAS.

Boil tender the peel of two large lemons pared as thinly as possible, changing the water two or three times. Take out the hard pieces and pound very fine. Beat half lb. of blanched almonds also, very fine, add one lb. of sugar, the yolks of eight eggs, and the whites of four and a lb. of butter, and mix all together. Line your tins with puff paste and bake in a slow oven.

Cracker Apple Pie.
Miss M. Moore.

Break in pieces one and a half soda crackers, or one *Boston* cracker, turn into a teacup of cold water, let it stand while making the paste. Put it in a pie plate with a little nutmeg, add a cup of sugar and juice of a lemon.

Lemon Pie.
Mrs. Walz.

The grated rind and juice of one or two lemons, three eggs beaten separately, one and a half cups sugar, two teaspoonfuls, flour, two-thirds cup of water. Beat the whites to a stiff froth, add three spoonfuls sugar, pour over the pie when baked and let it stand three minutes in the oven.

Another.
Mrs. Swalm.

Two lemons, two cups sugar, half cup molasses, half cup water, two eggs, two tablespoonfuls flour, piece of butter size of an egg. Crust with strips across.

English Apple Pie.
J. A. M.

Half peck greening apples, or sour apples, peeled and quartered, one pt. of sugar, half pt. cold water, twenty-four whole cloves. Line the sides of a deep pudding-dish with pie paste, invert a cup with a hole in the bottom, place in the middle of the dish, put in some of the apples, sprinkle some of the sugar, some of the cloves, then the apples, and so on; when all are in put in little pieces of butter over the top, then the water, cover the whole with pie-paste. Bake one hour and a half; serve hot.

Lemon Custard Pie.
Mrs. Thomas.

The grated rind and juice of one lemon, six tablespoonfuls sugar, one cup milk, one tablespoonful flour, yolks of four eggs and a little salt. Beat all together well and bake in a crust. While this is baking beat the whites to a stiff froth, add three tablespoonfuls pulverized sugar and a few drops of the lemon juice. When the pie is done, spread this on top in a merangue and set it back in the oven to harden and brown a little. Makes one pie.

Nice Cheesecakes.
Miss Cripps.

Three small dry sponge cakes soaked in a very little milk. Beat till quite smooth, and add three ozs. of butter (melted), the rind of a lemon grated, the yolks of two eggs and some currants, sugar to taste. Bake in pastry in small tart tins.

Pumpkin Pie.
Mrs. Thomas.

Pare and cut pumpkin in pieces of equal size, add half pt. of cold water and boil until perfectly soft. Put it through the sieve while hot. To one pie—one teacupful pumpkin, one egg, sugar and ground ginger to taste, sweet milk to give the proper consistency.

Fruit Pies.
Mrs. Sumner.

Squeeze a large lemon, boil the outside till tender enough to beat to a mash; add to it three large apples chopped, quarter lb. of suet, chopped, half lb. currants, quarter lb. sugar. Put in the juice of the lemon and candied fruits as for other pies. Make a puff paste and bake in patty pans.

Raisin Pie.

J. D.

One cup chopped or stoned raisins, one cup sugar, one cup water, two lemons, the juice and grated rind, two yolks of eggs. Bake and add merangue as for lemon pie.

Orange Custard Pie.

Mrs. Thomas.

Take one-quarter and one-half quarter of washed butter, the same quantity of sugar and beat together to a light cream, four eggs beaten very light. Boil the peel of an orange and pound it, and add the juice with half a glass of brandy, stir it well. Add a tincupful of bread and milk boiled together, beat well. Bake in crust.

Summer Mince Pies.

Mrs. Mason.

Four crackers, one cup chopped raisins, one cup hot water, same of cider, same of molasses, one and a half cups sugar, two-thirds cup of butter, one teaspoonful cloves, same of allspice, same of cinnamon, two eggs beaten and stirred in the last thing.

Peach Dumplings.

Mrs. Silleck.

Make as much good biscuit dough as you may require, cut in pieces as large as an egg, roll thin, have good juicy peaches washed and dried (not pared), lap the dough around them, sew in cloth and boil twenty minutes; the water must be boiling when you put them in.

Potato Pie.

One pt. mashed potatoes (prepared as for table), one qt. milk, one cup butter, two cups sugar, four eggs, nutmeg to taste. This will make two pies.

Cherry Pie.

Three cupfuls cherries, stemmed, one cupful sugar. Line a pie plate with paste, wet the edges, add the cherries, cover and bake in steady quick oven for twenty-five minutes.

CAKES.

REMARKS.

Making cake accuracy in proportioning the ingredients is indispensable. It is equally indispensable for the success of the cake that it should be baked as soon as prepared. It is useless to attempt making it light unless the eggs are perfectly fresh and the butter good. To insure success the following rule should be strictly adhered to, *except when directions are given to the contrary*. Cream the butter and sugar together, beat the eggs separately, then beat the yolks in milk, add to butter and sugar; sift flour and rub the baking powder through dry (or if cream tartar and soda are preferred, mix the former through flour, and dissolve the latter in milk), next add flour and baking powder, and lastly the whites beaten to a stiff froth, beat all the ingredients together thoroughly. Fruit must be well dredged with flour before putting into the cake to prevent its settling. To blanch almonds, pour boiling water over them and rub off the skins. To ascertain if a large cake is perfectly done plunge the blade of a knife into the center; for a small one insert a straw or the whisp of a broom; if in the least moist it should be left in the oven. If convenient to allow cakes to cool somewhat before removing from the oven it is better, as it prevents their falling. Molasses cakes should be baked in pans three inches deep.

Ocean Cake.
MRS. WALZ.

Whites of five eggs, half cup butter, two cups powdered sugar, one cup milk, three cups flour, one teaspoonful soda, two of cream tartar. Flavor to taste.

Vanity Cake.

MISS E. DORSCHEIMER.

Five eggs one cup sugar, half cup butter, one and a half cups flour; scant quarter of a teaspoon of baking powder. The jelly—Grate one lemon, two apples, add half cup sugar and two eggs. Beat the ingredients together, boil one minute, and spread between the layers of the cake.

Anise-seed Cake.

MISS CRIPPS.

Take one quarter lb. of fine flour, same quantity of cornstarch, not quite half lb. of powdered sugar, five eggs and a tablespoonful of well cleaned anise-seeds. Beat the whites of the eggs to a froth, add to it the well beaten yolks, then the sugar mixed with the anise-seeds, at last flour and corn starch. Use white wax for your tins instead of butter, take a teaspoonful of batter at a time, forming small cakes, and fill your tins, leaving a little space between them for raising. Bake in a very moderate oven. These cakes are delicious if baked rightly.

Rich Coffee Cake.

MISS CRIPPS.

Four cups sifted flour, three eggs, one cup milk, half cup of butter, one cup good yeast, and one cup of powdered sugar. Melt the butter, add the milk to it, have your flour ready in a bowl, put the three eggs into the flour, gradually add the butter and milk *lukewarm*, and lastly the yeast. Let the batter raise over night and early in the morning add the sugar, a small teaspoonful salt, one cup of currants, same of raisins, the rind of a lemon, one teaspoonful essence of bitter almonds and some citron cut fine. Put the batter in a well buttered round cake form, cover it over and let it raise again for one hour and a quarter. Bake one hour in a moderate oven. This cake keeps fresh for two weeks.

Spice Cake.
Miss Cripps.

One lb. of flour, a quarter of a lb. of butter, three eggs, three quarters lb. of sugar, one teaspoonful of baking powder, same of ground cloves, same of ginger, same of cinnamon. Stir the butter to a cream, add the eggs, then the sugar. Mix the spices and the baking powder with the flour and gradually put it to the butter, eggs and sugar. Roll it out on the pastry board, form into small cakes and bake immediately.

Chocolate Cake.
Miss W. Silleck.

Three eggs, two cups granulated sugar, one cup milk, half cup butter, three cups flour, three teaspoonfuls Royal Baking Powder. Beat the yolks in milk, add the butter and sugar beaten to a cream, then the flour and baking powder, lastly the whites of the eggs beaten to a stiff froth. The chocolate—One and a half lbs. Exposition chocolate (*Baker's sweet*), mix with a little hot water and the white of an egg, boil *almost* once. This quantity makes twelve *thin* layers; four to a cake.

French Loaf.
Mrs. Sharpe.

Two cups sugar, half cup of butter, one cup sweet milk, three cups flour, three eggs, one teaspoonful soda, two of cream tartar.

Jenny Lind Cake.
Mrs. Smith.

Two cups sugar, three-quarters of a cup of butter, two eggs, three cups flour, one cup of milk, one teaspoonful cream tartar, half teaspoon soda. Take out enough for two cakes, and add to the remainder of the cake, half cup raisins, two tablespoonfuls molasses, cinnamon, nutmeg, cloves. Make three cakes. Put together with jelly.

Delicate Cake.

Miss Cripps.

The whites of eight eggs well beaten, two cups powdered sugar, one half cup of milk, half cup butter, three cups fine flour, one teaspoonful cream tartar, same of soda. Sift the cream tartar and soda with the flour, add the eggs the last thing. For the icing take three-fourths cup of Baker's chocolate grated fine, three-fourths cup of powdered sugar, one tablespoonful vanilla, same of milk mixed together. Put this on the stove in a kettle of boiling water till thoroughly heated. Spread on the cake while warm.

Measure Pound Cake.

Mrs. J. Raymond.

Three cups sugar, two and a half cups butter, eight eggs, four cups flour, one teaspoonful saleratus. Stir the butter and sugar well together, add the eggs and flour well mixed, a little citron or mace may improve it. This cake if made light is very delicate.

Cream Cake.

Mrs. Smith.

Two cups powdered sugar, two-thirds cup of butter, four eggs, half cup of milk, half teaspoon soda, one teaspoonful cream tartar, three cups flour. Bake in layers, when cold spread the mixture between them. The filling—Half pt. milk, two small teaspoonfuls corn starch, one egg, teaspoonful vanilla, half a cup sugar. Heat the milk to boiling, stir in the corn starch wet with a little cold milk. Take out a little and mix gradually with beaten egg and sugar, return to the rest of the custard and boil, stirring constantly until quite thick. Let it cool before you season and spread on cake; flavor the icing with vanilla.

Delicate Cake.
Mrs. Chandler.
Whites of six eggs, half cup of butter, one and a half cups sugar, same of flour, half cup of corn starch, same of milk, one teaspoonful cream tartar, half teaspoon soda. Flavor with lemon or vanilla.

Cream Cake.
Miss Dorscheimer.
The cake—Three eggs beaten separately, one cup of sugar, one and a half cups flour, two tablespoonfuls cold water, two tablespoonfuls baking powder, essence to taste. Bake in two pie pans and split while hot. The cream—One pt. sweet milk come to a boil, two eggs, two tablespoonfuls (small) corn starch, let it boil until thick, stir all the time; when nearly done put in a small cup of sugar, and a small cup of butter, essence to taste.

Orange Cake.
Mrs. J. Raymond.
Half cup butter, one cup sugar, one and a half cups flour, half cup of milk, two eggs, two teaspoonfuls Sea Foam. Mix butter and sugar to a cream, add the eggs, then the milk, mix flour and Sea Foam together, and add it to the other and cook in layers. Jelly for the cake—Grate the rinds of two oranges and a lemon and add the juice of each. One cup sugar, same of water, one and a half tablespoonfuls corn starch. Boil the jelly, stirring continually. Get Messina oranges if possible.

Citron Cake.
Mrs. J. Raymond.
One lb. butter, one and a quarter lbs. sugar, two lbs. sifted flour, two lbs. raisins (pitted), half lb. citron, a wine glass of brandy, one teaspoonful saleratus, one pt. sweet milk and seven eggs. This makes two large cakes.

Cream Puffs.

Mrs. Reynolds.

Boil one-half lb. butter in one pt. of water, while boiling stir in three-quarters lb. of flour, then take it from the fire and stir in gradually ten eggs (not beaten), till quite smooth, add half teaspoonful soda. To be dropped on the sheets half the size you wish them when baked. Bake half hour. The cream—Boil one half pt. of milk; while boiling add four eggs well beaten in two cups of sugar and one cup of flour, this to be cooked together as boiled custard. Flavor with lemon, when cold drop into the forms for cakes.

Cream Puffs. (Blot.)

Two oz. of butter in a saucepan, with one and one-half gills of cold water. At first boiling throw in four oz. of flour and stir fast half a minute or so; then add four eggs, one at a time, or five if the eggs are small. Butter a tin, drop with a spoon one and a half inches apart, glaze with egg and bake. When done, cut—not quite through—and fill with cream. The cream —Two tablespoonfuls sugar in a saucepan with one of flour, three yolks of eggs, one-half pint of milk. Mix well cold, set on the fire, stir constantly five minutes and flavor.

Chocolate Eclairs.

Paste same as above for *cream cakes*, dropped on buttered tins lengthwise. When baked and cold cut through one side and fill with cream. The cream—One oz. of chocolate, melt it, add six spoonfuls sugar, yolks of eight eggs and two spoonful flour. Mix well cold, then add six gills of milk, place on the fire, stirring it continually till thick, flavor with vanilla; add a very little water to the chocolate, add to the cream, mix thoroughly. For the top—Grate four oz. of chocolate, four spoonfuls cold water, eight oz. sugar, stir on the fire, when a little thick dip the top of the cake in.

Hickory-Nut Cake.

MRS. SILLECK.

One lb. butter, same of sugar, same of prepared flour, five eggs, one gill rose water, one qt. hickory nuts *shelled*, one qt. English walnuts *shelled*.

Cocoanut Cake.

MRS. QUIRK.

Six eggs, one lb. of sugar, half lb. butter, three-quarters lb. of flour and one cocoanut grated.

Fruit Cake.

MRS. SILLECK.

One lb. butter, one and a quarter lb. sugar, same of flour, twelve eggs, wine glass of brandy, same of molasses, teaspoonful Royal Baking Powder dissolved in the molasses, one teaspoonful of cloves, two of mace, four of cinnamon; four lbs. raisins, three lbs. currants, two lbs. citron. Bake three hours in a slow oven.

Rich Molasses Cake.

MISS SWEET.

One cup *New Orleans* molasses, half cup butter, one egg, one teaspoonful soda dissolved in half cup of boiling water, two and a half cups of flour.

Marbled Cake.

MISS SWEET.

One cup butter, two cups sugar, three cups flour, four eggs, one cup milk, two teaspoonfuls baking powder. When cake is mixed take out one cup of batter, stir into it one large spoonful grated chocolate wet with milk. Fill pan an inch thick with yellow, drop in the dark. A little lemon added to the yellow is an improvement.

Jelly Roll.

MISS C. MIDDLETON.

One cup flour (teacup), one cup (scant) of coffee A sugar, three eggs, one teaspoonful cream tartar, half teaspoon soda. Milk enough to wet the soda and a little salt. Beat the whites and yolks together. Spread jelly on as soon as baked and roll the cake on a cloth.

White Sponge Cake.

MISS C. MIDDLETON.

Whites of five eggs, one cup of sugar, half a cup of flour, one large spoonful more of flour, half teaspoon cream tartar. Beat the whites of the eggs to a froth, then stir it in with the flour, next add yolks, then mix cream tartar with flour, beat lightly and bake in a quick oven.

Sponge Cake.

MRS. QUIRK.

One lemon, one cup sugar, one cup sifted flour, four eggs, yolk and sugar well beaten, then add the whites, then the lemon, little of the rind last, stir, *not beat*, put in the flour.

Crullers.

MRS. QUIRK.

Half lb. butter, three-quarters of a lb. of sugar, four eggs, one wine glass of brandy, same of milk, one nutmeg, and made stiff with flour to roll and cut in shapes.

New Year's Cake.

MRS. QUIRK.

Three lbs. sugar, two lbs. butter, one qt. cream, one wine glass of wine and one of brandy, caraway seeds and a *small* piece of soda; flour to make up, and stamp them with a print.

Cake Waffles.

J. A. M.

One lb. of butter, same of sugar, one and a quarter lbs. of flour, eight eggs, quarter teaspoonful soda, half teaspoon cream tartar, half of a grated nutmeg, a little salt. Cream the butter, then add the sugar, when *well* beaten to a cream add the yolks of eggs which have been well beaten, then the flour with soda and cream tartar sifted into it, the nutmeg and salt, then the whites of the eggs which have been beaten to a stiff froth. Bake in waffle irons on top of the range.

Spice Cake.

Mrs. Major.

Two cups sugar, one and a half cups butter, five of flour, one of milk, one of molasses, two teaspoonfuls cloves, two of cinnamon, two of nutmeg, one of soda, two of cream tartar, two cups chopped raisins, same of currants.

Cocoanut Cake.

Mrs. Avila.

Bake pound cake on long tins the thickness of jelly cake, spread each one with icing made rather softer than for a loaf, strew thickly with grated cocoanut and place one above another, four in all, drop in occasionally a spot of icing above the cocoanut on all except the top one, to make the cakes adhere better.

Hermits.

Mrs. Wilder.

Three eggs, one and a half cups of sugar, one cup of butter, same of chopped raisins, same of currants, one teaspoonful each of cinnamon, allspice, cloves and soda. Flour enough to roll out and cut like cookies.

Lady Cake.

MRS. AVILA.

One and a half cups sugar, half cup of butter, same of milk, two cups of flour, whites of six eggs, one teaspoonful cream tartar, half teaspoonful soda.

Jessie Cake.

MISS J. CROWELL.

Three eggs, one and a half cups powdered sugar, half cup of butter, same of milk, two cups flour, two teaspoonfuls baking powder, one teaspoonful of almond extract or essence of lemon.

Nameless Cake.

MRS. REYNOLDS.

One cup sugar, same of molasses, same of butter, same of milk, four cups of flour, two eggs, one teaspoonful soda, one tablespoonful cloves and cinnamon mixed, one teaspoonful saleratus, one lb. of raisins.

Gold and Silver Cake.

Whites of three eggs, one cup powdered sugar, half cup of butter, two cups flour, half a cup of milk, one teaspoonful cream tartar, half teaspoon soda. Flavor with almond. Gold with another flavor and yolks.

Jelly Cakes.

MRS. HOWARD.

Purchase *sugar cakes* at the baker's, select nice brown ones, spread the under sides very lightly with jelly and stick together. These are quickly prepared and must not be spread until about a half hour before eating, else they will become heavy.

Cocoanut Drops.
Mrs. Quirk.
One lb. of cocoanut grated, one lb. of flour, the whites of three eggs, three tablespoonfuls white sugar, the juice and rind of one lemon.

Hickory-Nut Cake.
Mrs. Swalm.
Half cup butter, two cups sugar, three cups sifted flour, four eggs well beaten, one cup milk, teaspoonful of soda in the milk, the meats of six qts. of nuts added when ready to bake.

Sponge Gingerbread.
Mrs. Swalm.
One cup butter, one cup molasses, two cups brown sugar, three and a half cups of flour, one cup water, four eggs, one teaspoonful soda, two of cream tartar, little salt and cinnamon.

Coffee Cake.
Miss J. Crowell.
One cup of brown sugar, one cup of molasses, half cup each of butter and lard, one cup of cold coffee, two eggs, one tablespoonful of cinnamon, same of cloves, same of grated nutmeg, two teaspoonfuls baking powder, one lb. each of currants and raisins.

Harrison Cake.
Miss Jennison.
One cup of butter, same of sugar, same of milk, half cup molasses, three eggs, one small teaspoon of soda, one lb. of raisins and flour enough to make as stiff as soft gingerbread, all kinds of spices.

Kisses.

Miss W. Silleck.

Follow directions for boiled icing, *make half the quantity*, place in small buttered tins for this purpose, and bake slowly.

Lemon Cake.

Miss J. Crowell.

Five eggs, three cups of sugar, one cup of butter, same of milk, four cups of flour, juice and rind of one lemon, one teaspoonful baking powder.

Crullers.

Mrs. Wilder.

Two cups sugar, three eggs, three tablespoonfuls melted lard, one and a quarter cups of milk, nutmeg and salt, two teaspoonfuls baking powder, flour to roll out soft, and fry in hot lard.

Almond Cake.

Mrs. Howard.

One lb. butter, same of sugar, same of flour, two lbs. of sweet almonds blanched and pounded, half a lb. of desiccated cocoanut, the juice and grated rind of one large lemon, ten well-beaten eggs and a gill of wine or brandy.

Watermelon Cake.

Mrs. Howard.

Take two cupfuls sugar, one of butter, one of milk, the whites of eight eggs, two cupfuls flour, one of corn starch and two teaspoonfuls baking powder. Take one-third of the batter and mix half a cupful of currants with it, take another third and add to it a little cochineal and a lump of alum the size of a pea dissolved in a little water. Flavor to taste and arrange in your pan as marble cake.

Lady Fingers.

Rub half a lb. of butter into a lb. of flour, add half a lb. of sugar, grate in the rinds of two lemons and squeeze in the juice of one; then add three eggs; make into a roll size of the middle finger; it will spread in the oven to a thin cake; dip outside in chocolate icing.

Pound Cake.

MRS. REYNOLDS.

One lb. of butter worked back to a cream, while beating add slowly one lb. of powdered sugar, ten eggs beaten to a froth, add gradually half a glass of brandy, one glass of wine and one lb. of flour, after which beat all well together for half an hour. Bake with an oven heat.

Brown Stone Front Cake.

MRS. L. SMITH.

One large cup of sugar, two-thirds of a cup of butter, four eggs, leaving out the whites of two for frosting, two cups of flour, two-thirds cup of milk, one cake of German chocolate (grated), one tablespoonful vanilla. Mix the chocolate in one half of the cake. Bake in separate pans and put together with frosting.

Old Lady Cake.

MRS. H. ZAHM.

One cup butter, one and a half cups sugar, three eggs, three cups sifted flour, one cup milk, half teaspoonful soda, one teaspoonful cream tartar. Beat the butter and sugar to a cream, then add the rest. Raisins can be put in if liked, if so, rub them in the flour; spice with cinnamon, just before putting it in the oven sprinkle sugar over the top. Bake in a slow oven.

Mountain Ice Cake.
Mrs. Chandler.

One cup of butter, two cups sugar, half cup sweet milk, three cups flour, whites of eight eggs, two teaspoonfuls baking powder in the flour. Bake as for jelly cake, in four layers. Icing—Whites of four eggs, eight teaspoonfuls sugar to one egg, one grated cocoanut.

Election Cake.
Mrs. Jackson, Boston.

Three full cups of dough, one full cup butter, two cups sugar, spice to taste, one and a half cups of raisins, stoned and chopped, two eggs, quarter teaspoon of saleratus, quarter of a cup of molasses.

Christmas Cakes.
Mrs. C. L. T.

Heat three qts. of molasses, one and a quarter lbs. of butter, mix well, then add quarter of an oz. of ground cinnamon, half oz. anise-seed, one teaspoonful cloves, same of allspice, three of baking soda dissolved in a little rose water, stir in by degrees four lbs. of sifted flour free from lumps, six ozs. of coarsely cut sweet almonds; when this mixture becomes too solid to be stirred it must be beaten with a wooden spoon for one hour, allow it to stand in a cool place for one week, then knead in enough flour to roll out as thin as pie paste, cut with small fancy pastry tins; bake a deep brown in greased pans in not too hot an oven; will keep crisp for months in a dry warm place in cake drums.

Hard Gingerbread.
Mrs. Kendall.

One cup of butter, two of sugar, three eggs, one teaspoonful soda, two of ginger, flour to make a stiff paste. Roll thin and bake.

Aunt Lincoln's Cake.

Mrs. Zahm.

One qt. of flour, one cup of sugar, half cup of butter, one egg, two tablespoonfuls yeast, cinnamon, allspice and cloves; mix stiff enough to knead well, when risen knead again, then put it into the pans and let it rise again. Bake a little longer than bread. When taken out rub over with a little milk and molasses or cream. Some like this baked in buns.

Loaf Cake.

Mrs. Cone.

Two lbs. of flour, one and a quarter lbs. sugar, one lb of butter, two eggs, half pt. yeast, one lb. raisins, nearly one pt. of milk. Spice to taste.

Plum Cake.

Mrs. F. Taylor.

One and a half lbs. of flour, three lbs. of raisins, two lbs. currants, one and a half lbs. sugar (brown), one and a quarter lbs. butter, quarter of a lb. of citron, two wine glasses of brandy, one teacupful molasses, same of milk, five eggs, two nutmegs, half oz. cinnamon, quarter oz. of cloves, one teaspoonful saleratus. Bake in round loaves in oven with heat suitable for bread *three hours*. Frost when cold. This cake will keep for months and improve by keeping.

Nut Cake.

Mrs. Roberts.

One lb. flour, same of sugar, three-quarters lb. butter, six eggs, two teaspoonfuls cream tartar, one teaspoonful soda, half cup sweet milk. Mix all the ingredients in the usual way; then stir in a qt. bowl of hickory nuts or English walnuts and a coffee cup of raisins.

Soft Jumbles.

Mrs. Hebert.

One qt. of flour, one teacup of butter, two teacupfuls sugar, three eggs, one teaspoonful soda, half cup sweet milk. Roll them out in sugar.

Delicate Cake.

Mrs. Hebert.

Seven ozs. of butter stirred to a cream, one bl. sugar stirred to a cream. The whites of fourteen eggs beaten, ifits eleven ozs. of flour, one teaspoonful baking powder rubbed in the flour, quarter teaspoon tartaric acid dissolved in a teaspoonful of warm water, and put in just before the cake goes into the pan. Measure out the flour and add the baking powder, putting in the eggs little at a time until all is mixed. Flavoring—Juice of a lemon.

Almond Macaroni.

Scald one lb. of almonds, take off skins and throw into cold water until all are done. pound them with two tablespoonfuls essence of lemon until a smooth paste, then add equal weight of powdered sugar and whites of six eggs. Mix well together with a spoon, dip fingers in cold water, form the mixture into small balls, dip fingers in cold water again, and pass over the tops, place in cool oven three-quarters of an hour.

Cocoanut Cones.

Mrs. Hebert.

One lb. powdered sugar, half grated cocoanut, whites of five eggs, whip the eggs as for icing, adding the sugar as you go on until it will stand alone, then beat in the cocoanut. Mold the mixture with your hands into small cones and set them far enough apart not to touch each other, place upon buttered paper in a baking pan. Bake in a moderate oven.

Jelly Cake.
Mrs. Hebert.
One lb. sugar, same of flour, half lb. butter, six eggs, one cup milk, half teaspoon soda, one teaspoonful cream tartar.

Spice Cake.
Miss C. Shirely.
One cup sugar, third of a cup of butter, one egg, one cup of buttermilk, one cup of raisins, one teaspoonful soda, three tablespoonfuls molasses, one tablespoonful each of cinnamon, allspice and cloves.

Feather Cake.
Miss L. Parker.
One cup of sugar, one tablespoonful butter, one egg, one and a half cups milk, same of flour (prepared), or one teaspoonful soda, and half teaspoon cream tartar, in plain flour.

Lady Cake.
Mrs. Valentine.
Two cups sugar, one cup butter, two cups flour, whites of eight eggs, ten teaspoonfuls of milk, one teaspoonful essence of almonds or the rind of two lemons, and not quite the juice of one. Stir the butter and sugar together, then add the milk, then flour, lastly the eggs and flavoring.

Walnut Cake.
S. B. D.
One lb. of flour, same of sugar, half lb. butter, five eggs, one cup milk, one teaspoonful cloves, two teaspoonfuls brandy, one tablespoonful baking powder rubbed into the flour, three large cups of walnut meats.

Queen Cake.
Miss Sweet.
Five cups flour, three cups sugar, one cup butter, three wine glasses of milk, five eggs, one teapoonful soda.

Jackson Jumbles.
Miss Sweet.
Three cups sugar, one cup butter, five cups flour, one teaspoon soda, one cup of cream or milk, two eggs.

Quaker Cake.
Miss Sweet.
Six ozs. of butter, twelve ozs. sugar, one lb. flour, half pt. milk, five eggs, two teaspoonfuls baking powder.

Cream Puffs, excellent.
S. B. D.
One pt. water, half lb. butter, three quarters lb. of flour, ten eggs. Boil the water and butter together, then stir in the flour, let it boil for five minutes, cool thoroughly, then stir in the eggs, one at a time without beating. Drop into a pan and bake from fifteen to twenty minutes. Center mixture —One qt. of milk, two coffeecups of sugar, one of flour, four eggs. Boil the milk, beat the sugar and eggs and flour together, stir with the milk and boil five minutes, flavor to taste, let it cool, cut open your puffs when cool, and put in the mixture. This makes forty-six cakes.

Imperial Cake.
Mrs. Parrott.
One lb. butter, one lb. flour, one lb. blanched almonds, one lb. raisins, same of citron, one nutmeg, ten eggs, one wine glass of brandy.

Sugar Gingerbread.

Mrs. Palmer.

Three eggs, two cups brown sugar, one cup butter, same of milk, ground ginger and a little lemon essence, salt. Mix stiff with flour and roll into sheets or cookies.

Orange Cake.

Mrs. Hulbert.

Four cups of powdered sugar, same of flour, one cup of water, ten eggs, two teaspoonfuls cream tartar, one teaspoonful soda, the grated rinds and juice of two oranges. Take out the whites of two eggs and put them with the grated rinds and juice of two other oranges for icing. Beat the eggs and sugar very light, add the water, then the orange rind and juice.

Snow Cake.

Mrs. Hulbert.

One tumbler of flour, one and a half of sugar, one small teaspoon of cream tartar, the whites of ten eggs. Beat the whites very light, sift the flour, sugar and cream tartar together and stir gradually to the eggs. Bake in a round pan (put paper in the bottom) about three-quarters of an hour. About ten minutes after it is baked, frost it with the white of an egg and three spoonfuls sugar well beaten, and cover with grated cocoanut.

Custard Cake.

Mrs. Valentine.

Two cups sugar, one of butter, one of sweet milk, one of corn starch, two of flour; four eggs, two teaspoonfuls cream tartar, one teaspoonful soda, flavor to taste. Make a soft custard and spread between the layers when cold. Stir the butter and sugar together, dissolve the soda in the milk, add the eggs and flour with cream tartar stirred in the flour.

Lemon Jelly Cake.

MRS. PALMER.

Cake—Half cup butter, one cup sugar, two eggs, two cups sifted flour, two small spoons baking powder, water enough to make a moderately stiff batter. This makes three layers. Filling—Put into a bowl half cup sugar, one egg beaten, juice and grated rind of one lemon, small piece of butter. Set the bowl in boiling water and stir frequently till the mixture is about the thickness of honey, when cold spread on the cake. Frost the top layer with white of one egg beaten to a stiff froth, and nine teaspoonfuls pulverized sugar.

Buns.

MISS B. JOHNES.

One cup molasses, one of sugar, one of butter, one of water, one and a half teaspoonfuls saleratus, two eggs, five cups flour. Drop from spoon into pan, one and a half teaspoonfuls cinnamon, same of ginger.

Molasses Cake.

MISS L. MIDDLETON.

Three cups molasses, one of suet or butter (suet is best), one of sour milk or boiling water, six of flour, two tablespoonfuls ginger, two teaspoonfuls soda. Beat well. This will make three tins.

Dried Apple Cake.

MRS. ROYCE.

Three cups dried apples soaked all night in cold water, chop, put on stove with three cups molasses, boil until soft, then beat three eggs, one cup butter, three of flour, stir in molasses when cool, one teaspoonful soda, some salt and spice.

Lemon Cake.

Miss Oakley.

One and a half cups sugar, butter size of an egg, two eggs, yolk of another, one cup milk, two cups flour, two teaspoonfuls baking powder, rind of one lemon. Bake in jelly pans. Icing—One cup sugar, juice of a lemon, white of one egg.

Doughnuts.

Mrs. Thomas.

One qt. milk, one lb. sugar, half lb. lard, five eggs, one teaspoonful soda, one pt. potato yeast. Mix all the ingredients together in a sponge in the evening and let it rise over night. In the morning knead it up and let it rise again. Then roll it into thick sheets, cut into strips with a jagging iron, twist them up and let them lie on a cloth well sprinkled with flour to rise again. Fry in hot lard and sprinkle with hot pulverized sugar.

Summer Pound Cake.

Mrs. Thomas.

One lb. sugar, half lb. butter, one lb. flour, five eggs, yolks and whites beaten separately, one teacup of milk, one teaspoonful cream tartar, one and a half teaspoonfuls soda, nutmegs, currants or raisins may be added, or it may be baked for jelly cake.

The Alphistera, or Variety.

Mrs. Thomas.

One lb. flour, half lb. sifted white sugar, four fresh eggs well beaten together, work it well into a paste, roll it out very thin, divide it into squares, cut it into strips and fry in hot lard of a delicate brown. The more the strips are curled and twisted the better, they should look like bunches of ribbons. Powder them over with white sugar.

Ginger Snaps.

Mrs. Thomas.

One teacup melted butter, two cups New Orleans molasses, three teaspoonfuls soda. Put the soda and molasses into the butter, add two tablespoonfuls ginger and flour to make a stiff paste. Roll thin and bake quickly.

Kisses.

Mrs. Thomas.

Stir together ten ozs. of loaf sugar, six ozs. of butter, spice to taste, a little sour cream and one and a quarter lbs. of flour. Roll very thin, cut out and bake, one teaspoonful soda dissolved in the sour cream. These are delicious.

Camp Meeting Cake.

Mrs. Thomas.

One pt. molasses, half pt. sour milk, half cup of lard or butter, one egg, one tablespoonful saleratus, spice to taste, flour to make a stiff batter. Bake in shells of pie crust.

Jackson Cake.

Mrs. Thomas.

Eight eggs, weight of eggs in sugar, weight of four in butter, weight of six in flour. Beat the butter and sugar to a cream, then add one egg at a time and beat thoroughly with the hand until all are in and it is very light. No flavoring.

Corn Starch Cakes.

Mrs. Kimball.

Half cup sugar, same of flour, quarter cup of butter, same of milk, one-eighth cup corn starch, one egg, three-quarters teaspoon of baking powder. This quantity will make eight small cakes. They will not keep long.

Cinnamon Bun.
Mrs. Thomas.

One cup mashed potatoes, one cup of the water in which they were boiled, two cups sugar, one cup butter and lard mixed, one teaspoonful salt, one cup potato yeast, one egg, flour to make a dough. At night set the sponge thus—one cup of mashed potato, one cup of the water, one cup of sugar, one cup of yeast (no flour). In the morning add the other cup of sugar (brown), one cup of butter and lard, one teaspoonful salt, one egg and flour to make a dough; when perfectly light cut slices off large enough to cover pie plates, by rolling with the rolling pin to the proper size without cutting around the edges. They should be less than an inch thick. Let them rise very light, then wash them well with melted butter and sprinkle thickly with sugar, cinnamon, and a little flour rubbed together. Bake in a moderate oven about twenty minutes. These are delicious for tea or luncheon, cold or fresh.

1, 2, 3, 4 Cake.
Miss Parker.

One cup butter (scant), two cups sugar, three cups prepared flour, four eggs.

Cream Sponge Cake.
Mrs. Ide.

Three-quarters of a lb. of white sugar, three tablespoonfuls water, boil together; seven eggs, two whites left out for icing and one yolk for custard. Beat whites and yolks separately, then together, then pour the boiling sugar over the eggs, beating all the time; beat this till cool, then add the juice of one lemon; stir in slowly half lb. of sifted flour. Cream to go between the layers—One tumbler milk, one tablespoonful corn starch, yolk of one egg, two tablespoonfuls sugar, flavor with vanilla.

Albany Cakes.

MRS. IDE.

One and a half lbs. flour, one lb. sugar, half lb. of butter, or less, two tablespoonfuls rose water, one teaspoonful saleratus in a cup of milk. Bake like jumbles.

Cinnamon Wafers.

MRS. MIDDLETON.

One lb. sugar, half lb. butter, three eggs, one cup milk, one teaspoonful saleratus.

Chocolate Cakes.

Beat the whites of two eggs with a quarter of a lb. of pounded sugar into a frothy cream, add the juice of half a lemon and six ozs. of finely grated chocolate. Drop this mixture in spoonfuls on a flat tin, and bake them slowly.

Strawberry Short Cake.

MISS G. HAWKINS.

Four eggs, reserve the whites of two for meringue, one and a half cups sugar, one cup milk, pt. prepared flour. Make in two layers like jelly cake, only thicker, leave the last one in the pan after it is cooked, then put in your strawberries well mixed with sugar, put on the other layer, then the meringues, the whites of eggs and one cup of sugar, place in oven and brown for a few moments.

Black Cake.

MISS THAYER.

One lb. each of butter, sugar and flour, one cup molasses, ten eggs, one lb. citron, two lbs. currants, three lbs. raisins (stoned), one lb. almonds (broken small), one teaspoonful cloves, two of cinnamon, one nutmeg (grated), half tumbler brandy. Bake four hours.

Fancy Cakes.

Miss Ducker.

White part—Half cup of butter, two and a half cups sugar, same of flour, half cup milk, whites of eight eggs, flavor this with almond. Yellow part and brown—One cup butter, two cups sugar, one cup milk, three and a half cups flour, yolks of eight eggs. To half of this mixture add three-quarters of a cup of Baker's chocolate. Red part—Half a cup butter, one cup red sugar, half cup milk, two cups flour (prepared flour use), whites of four eggs. Put in a pan alternate spoonfuls.

Leopard Cake.

Miss Ducker.

Half lb. powdered sugar, half lb. butter, the whites of eight eggs, half lb. flour. Dark part—Same quantity of butter, brown sugar and flour with the yolks of eight eggs, half lb. currants, four ozs. raisins stoned and chopped, one teaspoonful of cinnamon, same of cloves. Bake in alternate spoonfuls.

La Africaine.

Miss Ducker.

One cup sugar, one and a half cups flour, one tablespoonful milk, three eggs. Split the above and put this inside: Two and a half cups scalded milk, one cup of sugar, two tablespoonfuls corn starch, two eggs, piece of butter; flavor with vanilla. Cover top with chocolate icing.

Soft Waffles.

Mrs. Haxtun.

One qt. flour, one teaspoonful salt, one qt. milk, one tablespoonful melted butter, three tablespoonfuls yeast; when raised add three eggs.

Fig Cake.

Mrs. Mason.

One and a half cups sugar, two-thirds cup butter, whites of three eggs, one cup milk, three cups flour, one teaspoonful cream tartar, half teaspoon of soda; divide the mixture, and to one pt. add one tablespoonful molasses, all kinds of spices, one lb. figs cut up very fine.

White Fruit Cake.

Mrs. Mason.

Make up batter for a white or silver cake, strew flour and stir into it two grated cocoanuts, two lbs. of almonds blanched and cut up, and one lb. citron cut up in small pieces.

Almond Sand Cakes.

Mrs. Haxtun.

Ten ozs. butter, twelve ozs. sugar, yolks of two eggs, the white of one, a little cinnamon, one lb. flour, stir together and roll out like cookies, put blanched almonds on top, spread the other white over with a feather, then strew sugar mixed with cinnamon on top and bake. Delicious.

Sponge Cake.

Miss W. Silleck.

Five eggs, the weight of eggs in sugar, the weight of half the eggs in flour, beat the yolks and whites separately. Beat the yolks and sugar together till creamy, then the whites, when very light add flour, one teaspoonful (scant) of Royal Baking Powder mixed in the flour; do not *beat* after adding flour, mix gently. Bake in a very moderate oven.

Molasses Cake.
Mrs. Baker.
One cup of butter, two of molasses, one of water, one teaspoonful salt, same of ginger, one tablespoonful soda.

Snow Cake.
Mrs. Peet.
One and a half tumblers of granulated sugar, whites of ten eggs, one tumbler of flour, one teaspoonful cream tartar. Beat the whites to a stiff froth, sift the sugar in slowly, flour the same, cream tartar in the flour. Flavor with lemon, add a little salt.

Strawberry Short Cake.
Mrs. Jarman.
Three tablespoonfuls melted butter, one cup sugar, one cup milk, yolks of two eggs, one pt. of flour, two teaspoonfuls cream of tartar and one of soda; when baked beat the whites to a froth, put on top of cake and place in oven to brown slightly.

PICKLES AND CATSUPS.

Pickles.
MISS MOFFAT.

Make the brine of boiling water and salt sufficiently strong to bear up an egg, while hot pour over the pickles. Leave this on them a day and night, dry them on a waiter. Take a gal. of vinegar, one qt. of water, one oz. cloves, one of allspice, two roots of ginger, one oz. mustard seed. Let all this come to a boil, then add the pickles and let come to a second boil.

German Pickles.
MRS. WILDER.

Two hundred and fifty gherkins, one oz. allspice, half oz. cloves, one oz. mustard seed, one bunch of dill, one oz. coriander seed, three or four garlics, fifteen cents' worth bay leaves, six qts. cider vinegar, one bunch red peppers. Pour the brine boiling hot over the gherkins and let stand twenty-four hours. Then heat the vinegar with the spices and pour on pickles after wiping them out of the brine.

To Pickle Onions.

Peel and boil them in milk and water a few minutes, put cloves, spice, pepper and salt into your vinegar, boil them in brass, turn it on your onions and cover them tight.

To Pickle Cauliflowers.
MRS. MIDDLETON.

Scald a small bunch in salt and water, put in a jar and cover with vinegar.

Cucumber Pickles (never fails).

Miss Maxwell.

For one hundred cucumbers (small ones), take one pt. of salt and scald it in enough water to cover the cucumbers and let it stand twenty-four hours, then take from this brine, wiping each cucumber dry. Then take two-thirds vinegar and one-third water, scald it and pour over the cucumbers, let them stand ten days or two weeks, drain it all off and throw it away, as it has drawn out all the slime from them. Put on a fresh supply of clear vinegar which has been spiced, and have it scalding hot, add a piece of alum the size of a peach pit to make the pickles crisp. These will keep (as Marion Harland says, under lock and key) for any length of time.

To Pickle Peaches, Plums and Pears.

Mrs. F. Taylor.

Seven lbs. of fruit, three lbs. sugar, one pt. water, one qt. vinegar, one oz. cloves, one oz. cinnamon. Boil these ingredients, and pour over the fruit four mornings in succession, and the last morning boil the fruit until tender. Peaches and pears are always nicer for having the skin removed.

Peach Mangoes.

Miss Sweet.

Procure large, white, free stone peaches, rub them with coarse towel, and remove the stones. Have prepared grated horse-radish, mustard seed, black and white (whole) pepper. Fill the peaches and tie the halves together with stout string, Put them in a stone jar, pour the liquor over them, cover lightly with flannel. Liquor—One lb. light brown sugar, one pt. vinegar, and a little stick cinnamon. Let it come to a boil; stand ten minutes before pouring over the peaches. To one pk. of peaches about two qts. vinegar, four lbs. sugar, two ozs. cinnamon.

Tomato Catsup.

MRS. SWALM.

One bush. tomatoes, half gal. vinegar, one pt. salt, two ozs. black pepper, two ozs. ground cloves, two of allspice. Wash, boil and mash tomatoes, then pass through a sieve, being careful to keep the skins and seeds in the sieve. To the liquor that passes through add the vinegar and other ingredients. Evaporate it half away; then bottle.

Tomato Catsup, No. 2.

Bruise the tomatoes with the skins on, and boil them two hours. Strain through a colander, measure them, and to each gal. add four tablespoonfuls salt, four of whole cloves, four of allspice, two of cinnamon, two of ground pepper, and one half teaspoon of ground mustard mixed with some of the catsup, and put in just before it is done, and add half a cup of vinegar scalded in, at the last. Boil the whole steadily ten hours, or until it is of the proper consistence; you can try it by cooking a little in a saucer. When done strain out the spices through colander, and bottle tightly. This will keep for any length of time.

Pickle Sauce.

MRS. IDE.

One lb. of mustard, one oz. of turmeric (ground), one and a half ozs. allspice, one and a half ozs. whole pepper, one gal. vinegar, one qt. kept out to mix mustard and turmeric. The spice boiled in the vinegar must be tied in a thin cloth. The mustard and turmeric must be mixed smooth before adding to the rest of the vinegar. Then boil all together, stirring constantly to prevent settling. Add celery seed. This sauce is the perfect counterpart (if properly made) of the sauce resembling Crosse and Blackwell's Pickles, both in consistency and taste.

Pickled Tomatoes.
Mrs. Middleton.

One pk. of green tomatoes, slice them, reject end pieces, sprinkle freely with salt, let stand one day; add two ozs. of mustard seed, one of cloves, one oz. allspice, one of cinnamon bark, put all together, cover with vinegar and simmer awhile.

Chow Chow.
Mrs. Doubleday.

One half pk. green tomatoes, fifteen large onions, two large heads cabbage, twenty-five green cucumbers, one half lb. white mustard seed, one ounce celery seed, one half teacup ground black pepper, same of turmeric, same of cinnamon, one qt. small white silver onions (whole). Cut the large onions, cucumbers, tomatoes and cabbages into small pieces and pack down in salt over night. Drain off next morning and put the mixture to soak two days in vinegar and water; then drain and mix in the spices. Scald one and a half galls. vinegar with three and a half lbs. brown sugar and pour over the mixture while hot. Do this for three successive mornings, using the same vinegar each time. On the third day mix one lb. of English mustard with one half pt. salad oil and stir it well through the whole. Put it in jars and close tightly.

Piccalilli.
Miss Ducker.

One gal. fine chopped green tomatoes, four onions, mix the onions with tomatoes, and add one cup of salt, let this stand one night, in the morning squeeze them in a cloth dry as possible, then add one tablespoonful of ground pepper, same of cloves, same of allspice; half a pt. of white mustard seed, four teaspoonfuls ground mustard, six green peppers (not large) chopped fine, mix well, put in a pan with good vinegar to wet it nicely.

Cucumber Catsup.

MRS. HAXTUN.

To three large cucumbers peeled and grated put one onion chopped very fine, one pt. of vinegar seasoned with horse-radish, pepper and salt. Shake it up and bottle tight until you wish to use it.

Walnut Catsup.

MRS. HAXTUN.

Forty walnuts, one gal. of vinegar, two spoonfuls allspice, same of pepper, ninety cloves, two spoonfuls salt, one nutmeg, two spoonfuls whole pepper and same of horse-radish. Boil all fifteen minutes.

Cantelope Pickles.

MISS G. HAWKINS.

Take fine ripe cantelopes, pare and quarter them, cover with vinegar, let them stand twenty-four hours; then measure the vinegar, leaving out one qt., add three lb. of brown sugar, cloves, cinnamon and mace to taste, put vinegar and spices on the fire, when it boils up drop in the fruit. Cook from twenty to twenty-five minutes.

Tomato Condiment.

MISS HAWKINS.

Eight lbs. ripe tomatoes peeled, four lbs. brown sugar, put them in a kettle, stir and boil to the consistency of molasses. It will take from four to six hours to boil it. One qt. of cider vinegar, four teaspoonfuls mace and nutmeg, two lemons. Boil five or ten minutes, then put in jars.

SPICED FRUITS.

Spiced Currants.
Mrs. Titus.

Ten lbs. currants, eight lbs. sugar, powdered cloves and cinnamon to suit the taste, half cup cider vinegar. Boil an hour over a quick fire. Blackberries, raspberries and cherries are very good prepared in this way.

Spiced Plums.
Miss Sweet.

One pt. vinegar, three lbs. sugar, seven lbs. plums, one tablespoon cloves, same of allspice.

Pickled Peaches.
Mrs. Chandler.

Seven lbs. sugar, ten lbs. of peaches, one qt. of vinegar; all kinds of spices. Pare peaches, put sugar and vinegar with spices, and just enough peaches to cover till cooked. Boil syrup until thick.

Pickled Peaches.
Mrs. Wilder.

To seven lbs. peaches, three and a half lbs. white sugar, one pt. best vinegar, put vinegar and sugar in the kettle, when hot put in peaches and cook soft, stick three or four cloves in each peach. Plums in the same way.

Sweet Pickles.

P.

Four lbs. sugar, seven lbs. of fruit, one qt. of vinegar, use cinnamon, mace and cloves to taste. Make syrup of sugar and vinegar, with spice (whole), scald for three mornings and pour it over the fruit, and then put them in jars and cork up tightly and they are ready for use.

Spiced Cherries.

Take half a lb. of sugar to two qts. of cherries; boil vinegar, sugar, mace, allspice and cinnamon together, let it cool, then pour it over the cherries.

PRESERVES AND JELLIES.

Jelly.

Mrs. Reynolds.

To a package of Cox's gelatine add one pt. cold water and the juice of three lemons, let it stand one hour, then add two pts. of boiling water, one pt. of wine, from one and a half to two lbs. of sugar. Strain and pour into molds.

Crab Apple Jelly.

Stem the desired quantity of crab apples, put in kettle and barely cover with cold water, let boil until quite tender, after which strain through a bag, and to every pt. of the juice add one lb. of sugar, let it boil twenty minutes. Pour into tumblers after having first rinsed them with cold water.

Wine Jelly.

Mrs. Packer.

Put two ozs. of gelatine into a pt. of cold water with a doz. cloves and the rind of one lemon cut thin, let it stand half an hour, then add one pt. of wine, one pt. of boiling water, juice of three lemons, one and a half lbs. sugar; stir until thoroughly dissolved. Strain through a flannel bag into molds.

Currant and Raspberry Jam.

To every lb. of fruit add three-quarters of a lb. of sugar, boil about two hours, letting the currants boil half hour before adding the raspberries.

Orange Marmalade.

For this the Sicily or *any* sour oranges should be used. Peel the oranges very thin, and soak the peels twenty-four hours in salt and water (salt enough to taste *quite* salt). The next morning boil the peels until tender in fresh water, changing the water once or twice. Peel the oranges closely, throwing away the white skin, cut up the oranges into very small pieces, taking out the seeds. Cut the peels in small narrow strips. Weigh peel, oranges and juice, to every lb. allow one lb. or a little less of granulated sugar. Boil twenty minutes.

Orange Jelly.

Mrs. Chandler.

Soak in about a pt. of cold water one oz. of gelatine until soft, add the juice of six or eight sour oranges and the peel of four taken off very thin, and juice of one lemon, one lb. of sugar (or less if you like it quite sour), one qt. boiling water, and stir until the gelatine and sugar are dissolved, strain through muslin. Will make three molds.

Marmalade.

One pk. of quinces and two pks. of apples, pare and stew separately, take one lb. of sugar to a lb. of fruit, mix well and cook for one hour, stirring constantly.

Peach Jam.

Mrs. J. C. Smith.

Take ripe fine-flavored peaches, pare and cut them up, add one lb. of peaches to one lb. of sugar, or measure equally in a bowl, let the mixture stand over night and in the morning simmer it over a slow fire two hours or more until it is quite thick. Crack the peach stones, take out the meats, pour boiling water over them, rub off the skin, chop them fine, stir them in just before the jam is done.

Lemon Jelly.

Mrs. Swalm.

To one package of *Cooper's* gelatine add one pt. of cold water, let it soak two hours, to that add a qt. and a pt. of *boiling water*, two lbs. of sugar, the juice of four lemons. Strain through a coarse towel into jelly molds and set away to cool.

Cherry Sweetmeats.

A. W.

Take fresh, sour, bright red cherries, stone them and keep them as whole and perfect as possible, weigh them, and to every lb. of cherries allow one lb. of the very best white crushed sugar, make the syrup with just enough water to dissolve the sugar. When it has boiled clear put in the cherries and boil three minutes, then take all up, spread on large platter, syrup and cherries, and put in the sun for three days, or until the syrup is thick, take in each day before the dew falls, then put in jars for use.

Lemon Butter for Tarts.

Miss Sweet.

One lb. pulverized white sugar, whites of six eggs, yolks of two, three lemons, including grated rind and juice. Cook twenty minutes over a slow fire, stirring all the time.

Gelatine Apples.

Miss Sweet.

Peel and core apples, cut in halves, put in a kettle with one pt. water, sugar to taste, sliced lemon and green ginger, a little whole mace, boil tender. Then remove apples; put in the syrup one tablespoonful gelatine, boil five minutes, pour over apples.

Fruit Jelly.
Mrs. Silleck.

Have ready jelly prepared the same as *first* recipe for jelly, wet a mold with cold water, pour in a little jelly, next, on top of this, place either a bunch of grapes or bunches of currants, after which fill your mold with remainder of the jelly. When turned out the fruit forms a pretty contrast to the jelly.

Coffee Jelly.
Miss C. Middleton.

Four tablespoonfuls ground coffee to one qt. of boiling water, let it boil well (full ten minutes); enough water to cover half a box of Cox's gelatine, pour it over the gelatine and add one coffee cup of sugar; put in an egg-shell to clear the coffee, strain through a cloth into a mold; cream sauce flavored with vanilla. Use Borden's Condensed Milk in sauce.

To Make a Hen's Nest.
Miss W. Silleck.

Three large eggs, boil hard, take off shells, but do not cut them. Pare the yellow rind from six lemons, boil them in water till tender, then cut them in thin strips to resemble straw and preserve them with sugar. Fill a glass dish (a small and deep one) half full of nice jelly; when it is set put the strips of lemon on in form of a nest and lay the eggs in it.

Ambrosia.
Mrs. Merriam.

Have ready a grated cocoanut and some oranges peeled and sliced. Put a layer of orange in your dish, strew sugar over it, then a layer of cocoanut, then orange and sprinkle sugar, and so on till the dish is full, having cocoanut for the last layer. Prepare it two hours before you wish to use it. Pineapple can be substituted for orange.

Brandy Peaches.

Make a lye sufficiently strong to bear an egg, let the peaches scald in this a *few seconds* only, then put them into cold water for a few moments, rub off the skin with a towel. Make a weak syrup, weigh the peaches and boil them a few at a time in this syrup, until they soften a little, but not until they are entirely cooked; then put them on dishes to drain, while you add to the syrup sugar in the proportion of half a lb. to every lb. of fruit. Add only sufficient water to make the syrup, and boil a few peaches at a time in it. When you can pierce each peach to the pit with a broom splinter, take them out and put them into the jars. After all are done boil the syrup a few minutes and pour it out to cool a little; when it is cool enough have ready a bowl or pitcher in which to mix the syrup and brandy, allow half a pt. of brandy (white) to every lb. of fruit, mix thoroughly and taste the syrup; if not strong enough of the brandy to suit your taste add more. Pour the syrup over the peaches and close the jars tightly. Do not mix any more syrup and brandy than you have use for. In making the syrup be careful not to use too much water, as the juice of the peaches and the brandy thins it.

Strengthening Jelly.

Two ozs. of white sugar-candy, one oz. of isinglass, one oz. of gum arabic. Put these ingredients into a basin, cover them with cold water and let it stand all night; the next morning put it on the fire and let it simmer until all is dissolved. Then add one pt. of port wine and boil it all together half an hour, strain it and take a tablespoonful three times a day.

To Can Peaches.
Mrs. Ward.

Pare and halve the fruit; fill cans; dissolve quarter of a lb. of sugar in enough water to fill cans. Pour over fruit. Set cans in a large pan of cold water; put in oven and bring to a boil; if the fruit shrinks take one of the cans to fill the others. Cherries and all kinds of berries may be done in the same way.

5

Cherry Jam.
MRS. HAXTUN.

Three lbs. of stoned cherries, add one lb. sugar, let them stand three or four hours, then boil them about one hour, take them out and let your syrup boil till it is very rich, then put your cherries in and boil them down.

Currant Jelly.
MRS. HAXTUN.

Wash the currants and let them simmer in a preserving kettle until the juice is entirely extracted, then strain it. Take one lb. sugar to one pt. juice. Put the juice after straining into the kettle and let it *boil five minutes*, remove the scum, pour it on the sugar, as soon as the sugar is dissolved put the jelly in cups. Let it remain unsealed three days.

Chipped Pears.
MRS. LEAVITT.

Eight lbs. of pears sliced thin, eight lbs. of sugar, juice of three good sized lemons, and the peel cut in small pieces, one pt. cold water, quarter lb. green ginger parboiled first, as it is too pungent. Boil till the fruit is clear.

Raspberry Jelly.
MRS. THOMAS.

Dissolve two ozs. of tartaric acid in two qts. of cold water, pour it over twelve lbs. of picked raspberries and let it stand forty-eight hours, then strain it, taking care not to bruise the fruit. To every pt. of clear juice add one and a-half lbs. of superfine sugar, and when thoroughly melted stir it well and let it stand till a froth and scum rise to the top, which must be taken off before it is bottled. It must all be done cold, and kept in a cold place with bladders over the bottles, which had better be the wide gooseberry bottles, as if any scum rises it can be taken off. When used, dissolve one and a quarter ozs. of gelatine in a very little water, and add a qt. bottle of liquid jelly to it. Pour it free from sediment, stir it well and pour into molds. In summer it requires rather more gelatine. Strawberries do equally well, or any other fruit.

To Preserve Plums.

Pick over fruit; make syrup of brown sugar, clarify it when boiling hot and pour over plums. Allow them to remain in the syrup two days, drain it off, heat it to boiling, skim it and pour over again; let them remain in two days; then put syrup and plums together in a preserving kettle, and let simmer gently till syrup is rich. One lb. sugar to one lb. plums. Cherries or any other fruit may be preserved in the same manner. Put them in pots or jars.

Wine Jelly.
Mrs. Whitney.

One package of Cox's gelatine dissolved in one pt. of cold water. Let it stand ten minutes. Squeeze into it the juice of two lemons, strain out the seeds, one pt. of wine, add one qt. of boiling water, stir while pouring in, one and a-quarter lbs. white sugar, the white of an egg beaten light, and let it come to a boil. Strain through flannel; rinse the mold in hot water first, then in cold; wring the bag out of very hot water; do not squeeze it, but allow it to drip. In summer rub the white of an egg on the mold, that it may turn out smoothly. If these directions are followed your wine jelly will always be a success.

Calves' Feet Jelly.
Mrs. Mason.

Take four feet well cleaned, add eight qts. of water to them, boil till reduced to three pts., strain it through a flannel bag, when cold skim off fat from top and bottom. Then put the jelly into a kettle with one and a-half pts. white wine, three-quarters of a lb. of loaf sugar, one teacup of lemon juice, and the whites of eight eggs beat to a froth with the shells, mix all the above ingredients and let them boil one or two minutes, strain through a flannel bag until clear. If you want to color it take the syrup of violets, put in enough to make it blue, cochineal to make it red, tincture of saffron a yellow, and juice of spinach, green.

To Cook Apples.
Mrs. Mason.

Fill a qt. bowl with alternate layers of thinly sliced apples and sugar, and half a teacup of water, cover with a saucer, held in place by a weight, bake slowly three hours, let it stand until cold and it will turn out a rounded mass of clear and red slices, imbedded in firm jelly.

To Preserve Watermelon Rinds.

Pare off the green rind and the inner pulpy part, leaving nothing but the clear firm part. Have ready cold water, to a gal. add lump of alum size of an egg. Cut rind in pieces, according to fancy, throw into the alum water, cover with peach leaves, let stand in cool place till next day, turn off water, wash them clean, weigh them, to each lb. of fruit add half a lb. of white sugar, allow a qt. of water to each five lbs. of sugar, simmer over a slow fire until perfectly clear and tender, take off and flavor with extract of lemon and ginger.

For Grape Jelly.
Mrs. Haxtun.

Coddle your grapes, then take a pt. of the water to every lb. of sugar, and fresh lemon peel enough to make it taste. Boil until it is a jelly.

To Preserve Clingstone Peaches.
Mrs. Haxtun.

Get the finest yellow clingstones, pare them and lay them in a bowl, have their weight in sugar pounded and sprinkle it over them as they are put in, let stand two or three hours, put them together with sugar in a pan, add a little water, let the peaches remain until thoroughly scalded, take out with ladle, draining off syrup. Should there not be enough to cover peaches add more water, boil and skim it, return peaches, let simmer gently till quite clear. Have some stones cracked, blanch kernels and preserve them with peaches.

Canned Green Gooseberries.
Mrs. Ward.
Pick dried blossoms from the berries, place in cans and pour boiling water over, if the fruit turns white close cans, but if not, put the cans in boiling water and leave until the berries become white. These make pies equally as good as fresh fruit.

Cranberry Jelly.
Boil the fruit soft, strain it and add three-quarters of a lb. of sugar to one lb. of the juice or pulp.

Ale Jelly.
Mrs. Hobart.
One box of Cooper's gelatine dissolved in one pt. of cold water with juice of three lemons. Let it stand one hour, add three or four sticks of cinnamon; then pour on two pts. of boiling water, one and a half lbs. of sugar, three-quarters of a pint of ale. Strain into molds.

Rule for Canning Fruit.
Mrs. M.
Boil peaches eight minutes, 4 ozs. of sugar to one lb. of fruit.
Blackberries boil ten minutes, "   "   "   "
Raspberries boil six minutes,   "   "   "   "
Cherries boil five minutes, 6   "   "   "   "
Pears boil twenty minutes, 6   "   "   "   "
Plums boil ten minutes, 8   "   "   "   "
Grapes boil ten minutes, 8   "   "   "   "
Gooseberries eight minutes, 8   "   "   "   "

Neapolitan Jelly.
Make a qt. of jelly, separate in three parts, color one with cochineal, another with chocolate, the third with lemon, wet the mold, pour in a little lemon, then a little boiled icing, next a layer of chocolate, next icing, red on top of this alternate, until the mold is filled. Wait until the jelly is rather cool or it will run together.

Brandy and Preserved Pine-apple.
MRS. SILLECK.

Pare them, taking out all the little black spots; slice and core them; put the nice whole ones in a jar, first a layer of pine-apple, then a layer of powdered sugar, alternate with fruit and sugar, until jar is filled, cover with best white brandy, seal and they are ready for use. Take the broken pieces and cores, chop rather fine, add half lb. of sugar to each lb. of fruit, simmer till clear as amber, then fill jars.

Custards, Creams, Ices, etc.

Bavarian Cream.
MRS. TITUS.

One qt. of sweet cream, the yolks of four eggs, half oz. of gelatine, one small cup sugar, two teaspoonfuls vanilla or almond flavoring. Soak the gelatine in enough cold water to cover it for one hour, strain and stir into a pt. of the cream made boiling hot. Beat the yolks smooth with the sugar and add slowly to the boiling mixture. Heat again until it thickens, but not boil; remove and flavor. While still hot, stir in other pt. of cream, already whipped in a syllabub, churn to a stiff froth. The cream to be added one teaspoonful at a time and the mixture beaten to the consistency of sponge cake batter Put in molds and place on ice to form.

Apple Souffle.
MISS JENNISON.

Cover the bottom of a dish with nice stewed apples, sweetened and flavored to taste, pour over it a custard made of the yolks of eggs and milk; whip the whites with a little sugar to put over the custard and set in a moderate oven to brown.

Velvet Cream.
Mrs. Walz.

One oz. of gelatine, soak in one qt. of milk until soft, then place in farina boiler to scald, when thoroughly dissolved add one cup sugar and the beaten yolks of three eggs, with half cup cold milk, stir until it thickens and set away to cool, then add the whites of eggs beaten to a stiff froth. Flavor to taste, pour into molds.

Charlotte Russe.
Mrs. C. Vogt.

Take one qt. of cream and beat to a stiff froth. Previously to this put to soak half a package of Cooper's gelatine; add a pt. of cold water, then put on stove to dissolve, remove in a few minutes, and when cold beat to very stiff froth. Mix cream and gelatine together; sweeten with powdered sugar to taste, and flavor with brandy or vanilla. Set in a cool place.

Floating Island of Apples.

Bake or scald eight large apples, when cold pare them and pulp them through a sieve. Beat up this pulp with sugar and add to it the whites of four or five eggs previously beaten with a small quantity of rose water. Mix this into the pulp a little at a time, beat until quite light, heap it up on a dish with a rich custard or jelly around it.

Chocolate Icing.
Miss Sweet.

Quarter cake of chocolate, half cup sweet milk, one tablespoonful corn starch. Boil two minutes, remove from fire, flavor with one teaspoonful vanilla, add sugar.

Another.
Mrs. J. Moore.

Two squares Baker's chocolate, three-quarters of a cup of sweet milk, one and a half cups sugar. Pound chocolate and dissolve it on fire in milk. Then add sugar and boil slowly fifty minutes.

Pistachio Cream.

Take half a lb. of pistachio nuts, extract the kernels and beat them in a mortar with a spoonful of brandy, then put them into a pan with a pt. of good cream, and the yolks of two eggs beat light, stir it gently over a very slow fire until it becomes thick, then put it into a deep china plate, and when it grows cold stick it all over with small pieces of nut and serve it up.

Charlotte Russe.

MISS L. MIDDLETON.

One pt. of cream, one pt. of milk, quarter lb. fine sugar, four eggs, one paper gelatine. Dissolve the gelatine in the milk on the stove. Beat the yolks of the eggs and sugar together and mix them with the milk when cool. Beat up the cream and sweeten it, flavor with vanilla and mix with the rest.

Fairy Apples.

Have some tin molds about the size and shape of half a small orange, prepare some stiff corn starch, blanc mange, color half of it with pink sugar to a bright color, flavor the white with sherry wine and the pink with rose extract; dip the molds in cold water and fill half of them with the white and the others with pink, when cold turn them out and with a little gum water or sugar and gum water stick a white and pink together, thus making solid balls. Arrange in a pyramid on a glass dish.

Floating Island.

MRS. SMITH.

Boil one qt. of milk, stir into it the beaten yolks of six eggs, flavor with lemon or vanilla and sweeten to taste, whip the whites to a strong froth, when the custard is thick put in a deep dish and heap the frothed eggs upon it. Serve cold.

Pink Coloring for Icing.

Ten grs. of cochineal, same of cream tartar, same of alum, half gill of soft water, scald it, do not boil, strain and bottle it for use. A very small quantity is needed to color icing.

Apple Snow.
Miss Cripps.

Six ozs. of the pulp of baked apples, six ozs. of powdered sugar, the grated rind and juice of a lemon and the whites of two eggs, add a small pinch of powdered alum and whip together for one hour. Serve on sliced sponge cake or alone.

Dutch Flummery.
Miss Cripps.

Soak two ozs. of Cox's gelatine in a pt. of cold water. Boil till it dissolves. Strain and add one pt. of sherry or Madeira wine, add the juice and peel of two lemons. Beat eight eggs (yolks very thoroughly), and add sugar to taste. Boil all up together, stirring well, being careful not to overcook the egg. Pour into molds when almost cold, keeping it stirred previously.

Spanish Cream.
Mrs. Walz.

Half box of gelatine, three eggs, four tablespoonfuls sugar, three half pts. milk. Soak gelatine in milk, allow it to scald, then beat yolks and sugar together hard, stir both together, scald again. Beat the whites to a stiff froth, stir to the above, flavor and pour into molds. Make a jelly with the remainder of the gelatine and three lemons.

Flummery.

Half hour before dinner lay sponge cake or macaroons in the bottom of a glass bowl, pour over white wine until quite moist, make a rich custard with the yolks of eggs, pour over the above when cold; beat the whites of the eggs to a stiff froth and place on top.

Boiled Icing.
Mrs. Haxton.

One and a half lbs. sugar, half pt. water boiled till it ropes have ready whites of seven eggs beaten to a stiff froth, pour the syrup into a bowl and stir until milk-warm, then put in the eggs and beat for one hour.

Almond Custard.
Mrs. Ludlow Thomas.

Put a qt. of cream into a stew pan with a stick of cinnamon and a blade or two of mace, boil and set it to cool; blanch two ozs. of sweet almonds, beat them fine in a marble mortar with rose water and a few bitter almonds, if you like these flavorings. Add these to your cream, and after sweetening to your taste, set it on the fire, stir it till it is pretty thick, but do not let it quite boil.

Icing.
Mrs. Thomas.

Whites of three eggs beaten to a stiff froth, juice of one lemon, one teaspoonful of starch made fine, a small lump of gum arabic dissolved in the lemon juice, one lb. pulverized sugar.

Icing without Eggs.

Three teaspoonfuls gelatine soaked in water, just enough to cover it, when dissolved add powdered sugar and beat until it is the right consistency.

Angelic Fodder.
Miss B. Johnes.

One qt. milk, six eggs, six tablespoonfuls sugar, one glass of wine, a little more than half a box of gelatine, dissolve gelatine in qt. of milk, warm milk till gelatine is dissolved. Beat the yolks with sugar and pour the warm mixture over them. Heat to the consistency of boiled custard, let it stand to cool for eight minutes. Add wine and whites of eggs, cool in a mold.

Soufflé de Russe.
Mrs. J. Moore.

One qt. and a half pt. of milk, one oz. of Cox's gelatine. Boil one minute four tablespoonfuls sugar, three eggs, yolks well beaten. Stir into milk while boiling. Stir well and boil one minute, then stir in the whites of three eggs well beaten, take it up quickly, flavor with vanilla. Pour into a mold. Serve with cream and sugar.

Egg Cream.

Mrs. PARROTT, KEOKUK.

To three pts. of new milk use nine eggs, leaving out the whites of five, sweeten to taste, set the bucket containing cream in boiling water and let it remain until it comes to the right consistency, then let it become perfectly cold; when ready to serve take the whites of five eggs, four dessertspoonfuls of pulverized sugar and two of currant jelly, beat until it becomes perfectly thick and place on top of prepared cream. Tablespoonful at a time.

Delmonico Ice Cream.

Mrs. PARROTT, KEOKUK.

To two qts. of new milk use nine eggs and sweeten very sweet and cook in same manner as egg cream (see above). When ready to freeze add one qt. of pure cream and flavor to taste.

Charlotte Russe.

Mrs. WEAVER, UTICA.

Bake thin sponge cake cut in squares and place in molds or one large one hollowed out, which fill with a layer of wine jelly and currant jelly and stack up with whipped cream.

Rice Cups.

MISS SWEET.

Boil one teacup rice quite soft, sweeten with powdered sugar, place in small cups, when cold turn out, make a little hollow in top of each, whip the whites of five eggs with a little sugar, pour some over each *rice cup*, and spot on top and around the edge with currant jelly.

Chocolate Cream.

MISS SWEET.

One qt. sweetened milk, three tablespoonfuls of grated chocolate, two tablespoonfuls corn starch, when milk is scalding hot, add the corn starch and chocolate dissolved in cold milk. Boil five minutes, flavor with vanilla. Serve cold.

Orange Soufflé.
MISS SWEET.

Slice five oranges and pour over them a cold custard made of one pt. of milk, yolks of five eggs, sweetened to taste, beat whites of eggs to a froth. Brown carefully.

Chocolate Blanc Mange.
MISS L. MIDDLETON.

Half box Cox's gelatine dissolved in half pt. cold water, one and a-half pts. of milk put over to boil with half cup grated French chocolate. When the milk is just scalded pour in gelatine, sweeten to taste, cook twenty minutes, flavor with vanilla, pour into molds. To be eaten with cream, sweetened and flavored with vanilla.

Coffee Custard.
MRS. THOMAS.

Mix the white of one egg with one cup of fresh ground coffee and pour on it one pt. boiling water and let it stand ten minutes. Pour it off clear into a saucepan, add one pt. of cream and boil. Beat from five to eight eggs with one and a-half cups of sugar, and pour the boiling mixture over this, stirring it well. Set the whole in boiling water, and stir till it thickens. Eat cold.

Cream Glacè.
MISS M. MOORE.

One-third of a box of Cox's gelatine, let it dissolve in one pt. of milk on the fire, but not boil, then take the yolk of three eggs, half pt. milk, sugar to taste, beaten together and put in the milk after the gelatine is all melted, let it thicken as for custard, and separate in the spoon. Then take off the fire, cool a few minutes, strain it through a sieve, flavor to taste with vanilla and stir in the three whites of eggs (beaten stiff), just lightly, turn into wet mold. The jelly should be clear and go to the top and the rest to the bottom, if done correctly. It will fill two medium sized molds.

Tapioca Cream.
Miss M. Moore.

Soak one small teacup of tapioca over night. Put one qt. of milk to boil, take three yolks well beaten with one cup white sugar, and stir into tapioca, flavor to taste. When the milk boils stir the whole in, and when it boils second time, have ready the whites of eggs beaten to a froth, and stir in gently, pour off, set in cool place.

Boiled Custard.
M. L. T.

Boil one pt. milk with sugar and lemon, rind to taste, beat up three eggs, the yolks and whites separately, pour the whites into the yolks, then the boiling milk into the eggs, place the dish containing this (in which it is to be served) in a pan of boiling water and boil for three-quarters of an hour. The dish must be covered while boiling.

Brandy Cream.

One pt. of cream, the juice of two lemons, sugar to taste, two ozs. of isinglass dissolved in a teacup of water; whisk the cream a little by itself, then whisk in the lemon juice and sugar, then the brandy (a large wine-glassful), then the isinglass, strained and cool. If put in too warm it will turn the cream. This will fill two molds.

Caledonian Cream.

Two ozs. of raspberry jam or jelly, same of red currant jelly, same of sifted loaf sugar, the whites of two eggs beaten to a *stiff* froth, then beat the whole together and place on sliced sponge cake.

Carragreen Blanc Mange.
Mrs. Thomas.

A very nice blanc mange for summer use may be made by soaking a small handful of carragreen or Irish moss for a few hours in cold water, then boil it in a qt. of rich milk or cream; run it through a sieve, sweeten and flavor with vanilla or any thing preferred. Pour into molds and cool.

Ice Cream.
MRS. THOMAS.

To every two qts. of cream allow one well beaten egg and three-quarters of a lb. of sugar and two teaspoonfuls extract of vanilla, or any flavoring you like better. If the cream is not very good, the number of eggs may be increased and a little flour may be boiled in some milk to thicken the whole. Cream ought to double itself in freezing if well beaten.

Cream or Boiled Custard.
MRS. THOMAS.

One qt. new milk, one qt. cream, six eggs, one lemon. Beat the yolks of the eggs and three of the whites well. Let your cream and milk come to a boil, and stir in one full tablespoonful of flour mixed in a little cold milk. When it has boiled take it off the fire and stir in eggs and sugar. Grate in the rind and juice of the lemon.

Spanish Cream.
MRS. IDE.

Half box of gelatine, one qt. milk, yolks of three eggs, one small cup of sugar. Soak the gelatine one hour in the milk, put it on the fire and stir well as it warms. Beat the yolks very light with the sugar, add to the scalding milk and heat to boiling, stirring all the while. Flavor with lemon or vanilla, cool it before turning into mold. Beat the whites *just before serving*, to a stiff froth, add half a cup of wine and one cup of sugar. This makes a light froth to be poured over the mold. The whites will keep over night in a cool place in good condition, to be beaten up next day.

Apple Foam.
MISS THAYER.

Six good-sized apples, bake soft, take the pulps and put with it one teacup of granulated sugar and the white of one egg. Beat together until white and foaming, and the spoon will stand upright. It is improved with boiled custard poured over it.

Snow and Ice Pudding.
Mrs. Corwin.
In one pt. of boiling water dissolve one-third of a package of Cox's gelatine, three-fourths of a teacup of sugar, juice of two lemons, when nearly formed into jelly stir in lightly the whites of two eggs, beaten to a stiff froth, then place in a mold and serve with a boiled custard poured over it. Custard—Yolks of two eggs, one pt. of milk, two tablespoonfuls sugar, little vanilla.

Lemon Cream.
Mrs. Mason.
Beat the yolks of eight eggs, then put to them one pt. of boiling water, the rind of one lemon grated and the juice of two, sweetened to taste; stir it until it begins to thicken over the fire, and when a little cool put in glasses.

Chocolate Custard.
Mrs. Mason.
Dissolve gently by the side of the fire an oz. and a-half of the best chocolate in rather more than a wine-glassful of water, then boil it until it is perfectly smooth; mix with it a pt. of milk, well flavored with lemon peel or vanilla and two ozs. of fine sugar, when the whole boils stir to it five well beaten eggs that have been strained. Put the custard into a jar or jug, set it into a pan of boiling water, stir without ceasing until thick. Do not put it in glasses or a dish till nearly or quite cold. These, as well as all other custards, are infinitely finer when made of the yolks of eggs only.

Barley Cream.
Mrs. Haxtun.
Take two teaspoonfuls of pearl barley, boil it in milk and water till tender, strain the liquor from it, put the barley into a pt. and a-half of cream and let it boil a little; then take the whites of five eggs and the yolk of one, beat in with a spoonful of flour and two of rose water. Take the cream off the fire, mix in the eggs by degrees and set it over the fire again to thicken; sweeten to taste, pour it in cups and when cold serve.

Italian Cream.
Mrs. Mason.
Mix one pt. of rich cream with half a pt. of milk; sweeten to taste, add two gills of Madeira wine, one gill of rose water. Beat these ingredients thoroughly. Dissolve in boiling water one and a half ozs. of isinglass, strain it through a sieve and stir it into the cream; fill the molds, when firm turn out.

Floating Island.
Mrs. Mason.
Take one pt. of thick cream, sweeten with fine sugar, grate in the peel of one lemon and add a gill of sweet white wine; whisk it well till you have raised a good froth, then pour one pt. of thick cream into a china dish, take one French roll, slice it thin and lay it over the cream as lightly as possible, then a layer of clear calves' fee jelly, or currant jelly, then whip up your cream and lay on the froth as high as you can, and what remains pour into the bottom of the dish. Garnish the rim with sweetmeats.

To Whip Cream.
Sweeten a bowl of cream with loaf sugar and flavor it with any juicy fruit, or lemon or orange, by rubbing sugar on peel; set another bowl near the above, with a sieve, cover it, then whip the cream with a whisk, and as it rises in a froth take it off with a skimmer and put it into the sieve to drain, whip also the cream which drains off and when done ornament with lemon raspings. This cream may be used before it is set, upon custards, trifle or syllabub.

A Trifle.
Mrs. Mason.
Whip cream as directed above, adding a little brandy and sweet wine, then lay in a glass dish, sponge cakes and macaroons, wet thoroughly with brandy and wine, on top of this place a rich custard, grated nutmeg and lemon peel, next a layer of red currant jelly, upon the whole a very high whip.

Cream à la Vanilla.
MRS. HAXTUN.

One oz. of isinglass, five ozs. of sugar, three pts. milk. Boil the isinglass in the milk till it is dissolved, then take the yolks of four eggs well beaten and mix the whole, put it into molds, and when it is cold turn it out, it is better to be made the day before using it. Flavor it with vanilla.

Almond Icing.
MRS. HAXTUN.

Beat the whites of three eggs to a froth; beat one lb. almonds very fine with rose water; mix the almonds lightly with the eggs, and put in by degrees one lb. loaf sugar.

Cream Chocolate.
MRS. HAXTUN.

Take a little more than half a lb. of chocolate, grate and put in a kettle with three pts. of milk. Stir it over a fire gently until it looks smooth (only use part of the milk at a time), then add a little more milk and stir again over the fire. Continue this until it becomes the consistency of cream, sweeten to taste. Dissolve one box of gelatine, let it all boil about five minutes, strain, put in molds.

Orange Float.

One qt. of water, the juice and pulp of two lemons, one coffee cup of sugar, when boiling add to it four tablespoonfuls of Duryea's Improved Corn Starch mixed in water; let it boil, stirring it fifteen minutes; when cool pour it over four or five sliced oranges; over the top spread the beaten whites of three eggs sweetened, and a few drops of vanilla. Eaten with cream.

Chocolate Merangue.

Boil four ozs. chocolate in one and a-half pts. cream or milk, add three and a-half ozs. Duryea's Improved Corn Starch dissolved in milk; add four eggs beaten light with six ozs. sugar; when cooling flavor with vanilla. To be eaten with cream.

Chocolate Ice.

Mix two cakes of grated chocolate to a paste in milk; one qt. of milk while boiling, add the chocolate and sweeten with sugar to taste. Let it cool, then add one teaspoonful vanilla. Freeze as ice cream.

Lemon Ice.

Whites of six eggs beaten to a stiff froth; add the juice of five small lemons, qt. and a pt. of water, and very little more than two teacupfuls of sugar; stir until the sugar is dissolved. Fill mold and set in freezer.

CANDY.

Chocolate Caramels.
MISS L. IVINS.

Half lb. Baker's chocolate, two lbs. brown sugar, one cup of milk, quarter lb. of butter. Put all on together and stir constantly till it becomes grainy. Have pans buttered and pour in, when partly cool cut in squares with knife.

White Sugar Candy.
MISS L. IVINS.

One qt. of coffee sugar, half a pt. of water, dessertspoonful vinegar, lump of butter size of an egg. Boil one hour without stirring.

Molasses Candy.
H. W.

One qt. of molasses, a piece of butter the size of a walnut, grease the pot well and if any butter is left let it remain in the pot. Use a pot that will hold a gal., put in the molasses, boil over a hot fire, stir constantly when it begins to thicken; it is cooked when some dropped from a spoon will lay on a glass of ice water, take from the fire and stir in half teaspoonful soda. Pour in unbuttered flat tins.

Maillard's Chocolate Caramels.
Mrs. B. Johnes.
One cup boiled milk, one cup molasses or syrup, two cups brown sugar, half a cup chocolate, one tablespoonful flour. Cut the chocolate in fine pieces and when the other ingredients are well heated put in the chocolate.

Cocoanut Candy.
Miss Sweet.
One cocoanut grated, two lbs. finely sifted white sugar, whites of two eggs, milk of one cocoanut. Mix together, make into cakes. When dry it is as good as though boiled.

Toffy.
Mrs. Leavitt.
One cup sugar, same of molasses, half a cup sweet milk, one teaspoonful vinegar, one teaspoonful water, butter size of a small egg. Boil twenty minutes and when almost done put in half a teaspoon of soda. Turn into buttered pans.

Cocoanut Cream Candy.
Mrs. Taylor.
One cocoanut, one and a-half lbs. granulated sugar, milk of the cocoanut. Heat the sugar and milk rather slowly; when the sugar is dissolved boil rapidly five minutes, then add cocoanut finely grated, boil ten minutes longer, stir continually to keep from burning. When it becomes a rather firm paste on a cold plate it is done. Have ready buttered paper, lay buttered pieces of wood in form of a square, pour the mixture in, it will be soft at first, but will harden in two days if left in a warm dry place.

Lemon Drops.
Take the juice of three lemons, strained fine, and mix with it one lb. of fine sugar, beaten and sifted. Beat them one hour; it will make them white and bright; then drop them upon writing paper and dry them before the fire.

Chocolate Cream Drops.
Miss C. Shively.

Boil together two cups of sugar and one cup of water until it can be poured on a plate and beaten stiff; before removing from the stove flavor it with vanilla. After it has been beaten stiff roll it into little balls. Then grate part of a cake of French chocolate and moisten it a little with water, allow it to melt by placing the vessel which holds it in a pail of hot water, then drop the balls in, taking care they are well covered before removing them. Place them on a platter to dry.

Chocolate Cream Drops.
Miss Sweet.

Three tablespoonfuls water in a teacup, fill the cup with milk, two cups of granulated sugar; boil fifteen or twenty minutes, flavor with teaspoon of vanilla, remove from fire, beating it all the time until cool enough to roll into little balls. Grate two ounces of Baker's chocolate in a bowl, melt it over a teakettle of boiling water, roll the balls in, place on buttered paper and put in front of fire to dry.

Walnut Candy.

Make same as molasses, when done stir in either black walnuts or hickory nuts, or ground nuts.

Pop Corn Cakes.

Make good molasses candy, before pouring into pans add plenty of freshly popped corn, place in buttered tins and press down flat. Boil sugar to candy pop corn.

Vanilla Caramels.
New York Times.

Boil clarified sugar flavored with the essence of vanilla until it is very brittle, and then pour it out on a very carefully oiled sheet of tin. When sufficiently cool to receive an impression of the finger, mark it out in squares an inch in size, after which glaze them with another coat of sugar; then place them out in a dry place to harden.

To Crystallize Pop Corn.
NEW YORK TIMES.

Put into an iron kettle one tablespoonful butter, three tablespoonfuls water, and one teacupful of white sugar; boil until ready to candy, then throw in three qts. of corn nicely popped; stir briskly until the candy is evenly distributed over the corn; set the kettle from the fire, and stir until it is cooled a little and you have each grain separate and crystallized with the sugar; care should be taken not to have too hot a fire lest you scorch the corn when crystallizing. Nuts of any kind prepared in this way are delicious.

BEVERAGES.

Mead.
MRS. TITUS.

Three lbs. sugar, one and a-half pts. molasses, quarter of a lb. tartaric acid, two qts. boiling water. When cold add one oz. checkerberry, one oz. sarsaparilla. Dissolve one teaspoonful soda in one qt. ice water; when poured in goblet add mead until it foams.

Whipped Cream and Wine.
MRS. MIDDLETON.

Beat the whites of as many eggs as you need to a stiff froth, sweeten with sugar to taste and drop in glasses of wine.

Cream Soda.

Three lbs. of sugar, two ozs. of tartaric acid, the juice of one lemon, three pts. of water. Boil together for five minutes; when nearly cold add the whites of three eggs, mixing with them half a cup of flour, and beating the eggs well; add also half oz. of essence of wintergreen. For use—Put a small wineglassful into half a tumbler of water, and add a small teaspoonful of carbonate of soda. When carefully bottled, this will keep for months.

Currant Wine.
Miss Cripps.

To every qt. of currant juice three qts. of water and three lbs. of white sugar. Put all in a small cask and mix well. Do not bung it up, but put in the cork lightly. About half a pt. of brandy or whisky to five gals. of wine. Let it work for three or four weeks, then bung the cask tight, and keep for one year. An extra qt. of currant juice to every five gals. is an improvement. The cask must be sufficiently full for the working of the wine to come out at the top.

Milk Punch.
Mrs. Hebert.

One wine glass of brandy, two teaspoonfuls sugar, two-thirds goblet of milk, quantity of chopped ice. Put the contents into a tin muddler, and shake thoroughly for three minutes. The glass must fit the muddler tightly to exclude the air.

Blackberry Brandy.
Miss Sweet.

To one pk. of berries, well mashed, add two ozs. allspice, one oz. cinnamon, one oz. cloves; mix and boil slowly until well cooked; then strain the juice through flannel and add to each pt. of juice one lb. loaf sugar. Boil again for some time and while cooking add one qt. best *Cognac brandy*.

Egg-Nogg.

Beat six eggs separately, stir the yolks into one qt. of milk, or thin cream, half lb. of sugar, mix in half pt. rum or brandy; flavor with a grated nutmeg; lastly stir in the beaten whites of three eggs. Mix in a china bowl.

Pie-Plant Wine.
Mrs. Middleton.

Chop the plant fine, put in a jar, cover it with water, let it stand twenty-four hours, then strain. Then put to a gal. of juice three and a-half lbs. of white sugar, put in a jug until it sinks, then strain it off and cork tight.

To Make Rennet Wine.
Mrs. Leavitt.
Half a rennet cut in small fine pieces and put in a qt. of wine, one oz. stick cinnamon, one grated nutmeg. Shake occasionally for a few days, when it will be fit for use.

Raspberry Vinegar.
Miss Cripps.
To three lbs. of raspberries add one pt. and a-half of the best vinegar. Let the vinegar stand on the berries for three or four days; then stir them well together and strain. To every pt. of juice add one and a-half lbs. of white sugar. Boil three-quarters of an hour.

Orange Lemonade.
Take three oranges, one large lemon and two or three ozs. of sugar; rub off some of the peel on to the sugar, squeeze on the juice and pour on two pts. of boiling water; mix the whole and strain.

Measure for Liquids.
Sixteen large tablespoonfuls are half a pt.; eight large tablespoonfuls are one gill; four large tablespoonfuls are half a gill; two gills are half a pt.; two pts. are one qt.; four qts. are one gal.; a common sized tumbler holds half a pt.; a common sized wine-glass holds half a gill; four teaspoonfuls are one tablespoonful.

Apple Jack.
Mrs. Haxtun.
Eight apples baked, two lbs. white sugar, one pt. brandy, half pt. Jamaica rum, two qts. hot water, one nutmeg, one lemon, sliced thin. Bake the apples and mash them skin and all, add the sugar and pour on the hot water; when cold add the liquor, nutmeg and lemon. Improve by keeping a few days.

Punch.
MRS. HAXTUN.

Half gal. of cold green tea, three pts. Jamaica rum, one pt. of brandy, one pt. of sherry wine, one qt. of water, two cups of white sugar to one of currant jelly. Cut crosswise six lemons.

Lemonade.

Dissolve sugar in lemon juice, at little at a time, dilute with water to suit the taste, add a large piece of ice, a few slices of lemon, berries and small pieces of pine-apple if desired.

Gum Arabic Water.
MRS. ANNAN.

Two ozs. gum arabic, same of rock candy, six lumps of block sugar, juice of two lemons, one pt. of boiling water; stir occasionally until dissolved. Will be enough for two days.

Apple Water.
MRS. ANNAN.

Six nice apples sliced thin without peeling, juice of one lemon and one qt. of boiling water, sweeten to taste and let it stand until cold. This is a very refreshing drink in cases of fever.

Cherry Bounce.

Add three lbs. loaf sugar, two ozs. bitter almonds to six lbs. of cherries; two qts. best brandy poured over this, let it steep, then bottle. Can either strain or leave the cherries in.

Claret Cup.
NEW YORK TIMES.

Six tablespoonfuls sherry, two tablespoonfuls brandy, one and a half ozs. sugar. a few shreds lemon peel; to these add one bottle claret and one bottle soda-water. Keep in a cool place and only open before drinking.

MISCELLANEOUS.

To Wash Bankets.
MRS. LEAVITT.

Take a pt. of soft soap, put into it a desertspoonful of powdered borax, pour boiling water upon it until the soap is dissolved, then mix it well in a tub of cold water, enough to cover the blankets well, let them soak for one hour of more and occasionally pull the blankets up and down to stir them, but do not rub them. After they have been in the water until it looks as if the dirt was out, put them into a tub of cold clear water without wringing them, then after soaking and moving about a little put them into a tub of clean cold water and let them soak a while, then lay then over a double line in the yard; do not wring them, let them drip and they will be soft and white when dried. This quantity will wash one pair of small blankets, or one large one.

Taking out Iron-Rust.
MISS C. MIDDLETON.

Place cream tartar on spot, moisten with water.

To Clean Gold Chains.
MISS CARRIE SHIVELY.

Put the chain in a small glass bottle with water, a little tooth-powder and some soap. Cork the bottle and shake it violently. The friction against the glass polishes the gold, and the soap and powder extract dirt from the chain. Rinse in clear cold water, wipe with towel and the polish will surprise you.

Flaxseed Poultice.

If a flaxseed poultice is required to heal, add a few drops of laudanum; if to draw, use cream tartar instead.

Chapped Hands.
MRS. MIDDLETON.
Ten cents' worth of glycerine, five cents' worth of borax, dissolved in one pt. of hot water and perfumed with rose-water.

Asthma Cure.
MRS. J. HEBERT.
Twenty grains tartar emetic, forty grains pulverized opium, four ozs. spirits sweet niter, two ozs. liquorice, twelve tablespoonfuls honey, one pt. BEST whisky. A dessertspoonful to be taken three times a day.

For Cleaning Silver. Poison.
MRS. J. HEBERT.
Dissolve one-half lb. cyanide of potassium and one half lb. salts of tartar in one gallon soft water. Dip the article in the solution for a *few seconds only*. Wash with clean hot water, wipe dry with soft towels and chamois skin.

To Wash Hair Brush.
Washing soda dissolved in water, place bristles of brush in (careful not to allow the water to reach the wood or ivory), let stand a few moments. Dip in clean water and dry in the sun.

To Clean a Fine Tooth Comb.
Fasten several lengths of strong silk or cotton to a bureau handle; hold the comb in the left hand, pass the thread between the teeth of the comb. Wash well and dry with soft towel.

An Excellent Wash for the Hair.
One handful of bran in one qt. of water, cool and strain, when milk-warm rub in a little white soap (castile), wash the hair thoroughly, part the hair to reach the roots; beat the yolk of an egg and with your fingers rub into the roots well, allow it to remain a few minutes; then rinse your hair in clear water, wipe dry. Use the above once a fortnight.

Poultice, which will not blister.
MRS. MIDDLETON.
Beat the white of an egg, mix mustard with it.

Java Water, for Removing Mildew.
MISS B. JOHNES.
Take two gals. rain water, pour it boiling hot upon one lb. sal-soda and half lb. chloride of lime and let it stand over night. Then pour off the water clear and bottle it for use. Use one and a-half pts. to one gal. of water. The article may remain in this one hour or more.

Cologne.
MISS MOFFAT.
One oz. oil of bergamot, one oz. oil of lemon, two drachms oil of neroly, one drachm oil or ottar of roses, two drachms of musk, sixteen drops oil of cinnamon, twelve drops oil of cloves. The musk powder must be put in a gill of alcohol; after a few weeks the decoction can be poured off and alcohol again applied. This will make one gal.

The odor may be prevented from escaping by keeping the cork and neck of the bottle covered with the finger-end or thumb of an old kid glove cut off for that purpose.

Cleaning Gloves.
MISS L. SILLECK.
Fill a glass half full of clear benzine, immerse the glove, squeeze it gently once or twice, then draw on the hand (or place on a cloth), rub quickly and softly with clean white towel. When clean place near *register* to dry, as the heat destroys the obnoxious odor. (*Never take benzine in a room where there is an open fire.*) This quantity will clean two pairs.

Insects in Cages.
Put a piece of linen once or twice doubled over the top and let hang down the sides of the cage every night, you will find it full of insects in the morning. Wash the linen each day in hot water to kill the insects.

To Remove Grease from Silk.
MISS L. MIDDLETON.

Wash soiled part with ether.

To Cure a Felon.
Cranberries (raw) mashed and applied as a poultice to a felon, will in almost all cases prove effective.

Something Worth Knowing.
If after having bruised some sprigs of parsley in your hands you attempt to rinse glasses, they will suddenly snap or break.

To Wash Navy-Blue Woolen Stockings.
Soak them ten minutes, before washing them, in a pail of cold water containing one teaspoonful of sugar of lead, wash in weak borax water. Never use much soap in washing, it hardens the wool.

To Crystallize Grasses and Twigs.
Twelve ozs. of alum dissolved in two qts. of boiling water, tie grasses in a bunch and place in solution while hot, let it remain without touching it until cold, then separate grasses; cover a twig by wrapping some loose wool or cotton round the branches, tie it on with worsted. Suspend this in a basin or jar, dissolve alum in boiling water and pour it over. Allow it to stand twelve hours; wire baskets can be covered in the same manner. If the crystals are too large make the solution weaker.

Billiousness.
Oranges ward off billious attacks: eat three oranges a day and the doctors would lose their most profitable cases.

Borax for Washing.
MRS. HAXTUN.

Woolens washed in cold water with a little borax will not only be well cleaned but there will be no shrinkage. The women of Holland, so noted for their white clothes, use borax in the proportion of a large handful to about ten gals. of boiling water.

To Clean Black Lace.
An even teaspoon of borax in a pint of warm water, place lace on clean black cloth, sponge with black kid glove, cover with black silk and iron while damp.

For Ivies.
Mrs. Mason.

Put rusty nails into the earth, water once a week with tobacco water, put a sweet potato in the water.

For Chest and Lung Complaints.
Mrs. Mason.

Take one qt. of freshly skimmed milk, boil in it one oz. of manna, drinking this quantity cool in small draughts at intervals through the day.

For Sickness at Stomach.
Pop corn freshly popped and salted; sometimes a glass of kissengen will ward off a sick-headache.

Polish for Walnut Furniture.
Mrs. Haxtun.

One pt. of shellac, half a pt. of French varnish and a very little boiled oil. Shake the mixture well before using it, dampen a piece of soft cloth or cotton, rub the furniture; then rub dry with another piece of cloth. (This is used only for walnut furniture.)

Wash for the Hair.
Three pts. of bay rum, half pt. spirits of wine, half pt. of water, quarter of an oz. of tincture of cantharides, quarter of an oz. carbonate of ammonia, half oz. salt of tartar, rub it on the head after washing with water.

Toilet.
Glycerine well rubbed in with the hand, then magnesia, wipe with fine towel.

For Cleaning Paint.
Use ammonia and water.

To Make Linen Glossy.

Take the solid mutton fat, render it and add one teaspoonful sugar, throw it into cold water, and use it instead of butter or wax in starch.

Tooth Powder.

Use prepared chalk.

Compress for Sprains.

Wet a cloth thoroughly with ice water, bind it around the sprain closely; wrap outside of this flannel (dry). Apply until relief is found.

Antidote To Poison.

For any poison swallow instantly a glass of cold water with a heaping teaspoonful of common salt, and one of ground mustard stirred in. This is a speedy emetic. When it has acted swallow the whites of two raw eggs. If you have taken corrosive sublimate take half a dozen raw eggs besides the emetic. If laudanum, a cup of very strong coffee. If arsenic, first the emetic, then half a cup of sweet oil or melted lard.

To Stop the Flow of Blood.

MARION HARLAND.

Bind the cut with a cobweb and brown sugar pressed on like lint, or if you cannot obtain these, with the fine dust of tea. Apply laudanum when the blood ceases to flow.

Eau Sucre.

MARION HARLAND.

Dissolve three or four lumps of loaf sugar in a glass of ice water, and take a teaspoonful every few minutes for a tickling in the throat. Keep it ice cold.

White Liniment for Rheumatism.

MRS. HAXTON.

The yolk of one egg, a wine-glass of vinegar, same of water, wine-glass and a-half of turpentine, put them into a bottle, as they are put *down* and shake them well.

Items for Housekeepers.
Mrs. Haxtun.

Alum or vinegar is good to set colors of red, green, or yellow. A hot shovel held over burnished furniture will take out white spots. A bit of glue dissolved in skimmed milk and water, will restore rusty old crape. If your flat irons are rough, rub them with fine salt and it will make them smooth. Soap rubbed on the hinges of doors will prevent their creaking. Scotch snuff put on the holes where crickets come out will destroy them. Wood ashes and common salt, wet with water, will stop the cracks of a stove, and prevent the smoke from escaping.

Cure for Small-Pox and Scarlet Fever.
New York Times

Sulphate of zinc, one gr.; foxglove (digitalis), one gr.; half teaspoon of sugar; mix with two tablespoonfuls water. When thoroughly mixed add four ozs. of water. Take a spoonful every hour. Either disease will disappear in twelve hours. For a child smaller doses, according to age. A correspondent of the Stockton (Cal.) *Herald* claims to have personally known of hundreds of cases of the successful use of this receipt for small-pox, and says that it will prevent or cure the disease though the pitting be filling. It is harmless if taken by a well person.

For Roaches.
Mrs. Mason.

Borax powder sprinkled plentifully around the kitchen closets will almost completely exterminate roaches. It is perfectly harmless in case it should accidentally come in contact with food.

To Clean Marble.
New York Times.

Take two parts common soda, one part pulverized pumice-stone, one part finely-powdered chalk; sift the mixture through a fine sieve and then mix with water; rub it thoroughly over the surface of the marble, and the stains will be removed; then wash the marble over with soap and water.

Earache.

There is scarcely any ache to which children are subject so hard to bear and difficult to cure as the earache. But this remedy is said never to fail. Take a piece of cotton batting, put upon it a pinch of black pepper, gather it up and tie it, dip in sweet oil and insert into the ear. Put a flannel bandage over the head to keep it warm. It will give immediate relief.

DINNER, LUNCH AND TEA.

Remarks.

Only a housekeeper can appreciate the annoyance of the ever-recurring query, "What shall we have for breakfast, dinner and tea?" The inventive genius of the household head is exercised in varying dishes for every meal ; in this and in other respects the intention has been to compile a work for *practical* use; also giving hints for setting table, etc. The custom of having a waiter or waitress retire after the first wants are attended to at breakfast, lunch and tea insures privacy and sociality at those comfortable meals. Waiting at dinner is far the most important matter connected with a servant's duty, upon it depends not only the comfort of the host and hostess but that of the guests. What sooner will produce an ill-at-ease feeling than a nervous exchange of glances between hostess and servant ? Avoid it! Laying a cloth is the first thing done; a baize placed underneath gives a richer and heavier look to the tablecloth; that it may not present a tumbled appearance care is required in opening it. What more inducive to a good appetite than a prettily arranged table? Flowers add very materially to the beauty of it, and when used as a center-piece is oftentimes surrounded by fancy dessert dishes. A plate, knife and fork to each person, a folded napkin on each plate, on this a piece of bread about a finger in length and one inch thick, glasses for water and wine—the former should be filled just before the guests enter the room. Fancy spoons placed at either end of the table; at the side of these, salt and pepper stands. Plates should be arranged for each course; on dessert plate fold a fruit napkin, a finger bowl (on top of napkin) half full of water with a slice of lemon in it. Guests being announced, place soup tureen and soup plates in front of hostess; then follow the different courses. It is not essential to use the crumb-brush until after the course preceding dessert. Coffee is served either with or directly after dessert. The hostess gives the signal for retiring.

Breakfast Parties

Vary but little from dinner-giving; silver service remains on table during entire meal. The fashionable time is between the hours of ten and twelve.

Lunch Parties

Are rapidly becoming formal affairs. Differ from dinner in so far as having meats and poultry already carved and placed on platters garnished with lettuce leaves; entrées on china or glass shells. It is not incumbent to delay any meal for an invited guest longer than ten minutes.

BILLS OF FARE.

BREAKFAST (without invited guests).

WINTER BREAKFAST.

Chocolate—Tea—Coffee.
Oatmeal Porridge—Rice Croquettes.
Beefsteak—Saratoga Potatoes.
Fried Oysters—Omelette.
Parker House Rolls—Corn Muffins.
Griddle Cakes.

SUMMER BREAKFAST.

Melons—Peaches.
Coffee—Tea—Cocoa.
Boiled Rice—Hominy.
Broiled Chicken—Stewed Potatoes.
Lamb Chops—Corn Oysters.
Pop Overs—Biscuit.
Waffles.

TEA.

WINTER TEA.
Coffee—Tea.
Soda Biscuit.
Veal Loaf—Lobster Salad—Raw Oysters.
Brandy Peaches—Coffee Jelly—Cream.
Cake.

SUMMER TEA.
Coffee—Tea.
Pickled Salmon—Chicken Salad.
Pressed Tongue.
Tea Biscuit—Waffles.
Berries—Cream—Cake.

DINNER.

WINTER DINNER.
Mullagatawny Soup.
Turbot à la Creme.
Roast Beef—Chicken Croquettes—Roast Turkey.
Cranberry Sauce—Celery.
Mashed Potatoes—Sweet Potatoes.
Stewed Tomatoes—Macaroni.
Boiled Onions.

DESSERT.
Chocolate Pudding.
Mince Pie—Cheese.
Charlotte Russe—Fruits.
Nuts—Coffee.

SUMMER DINNER.
Vermicelli Soup.
Scalloped Lobster or Salmon—Green Corn Pudding.
Roast Lamb—Boiled Chicken—Baked Ham.
Mint Sauce—Currant Jelly—Lettuce.
Asparagus—Green Peas.
Succotash—Mashed Potatoes.
Scalloped Oysters.

DESSERT.
Lemon Pudding—German Toast.
Cherry Pie—Cheese.
Cream Glacè—Wine Jelly.
Ices—Fruit—Coffee.

LUNCH PARTIES.

WINTER LUNCH.

Oyster Stew.
Sliced Turkey (garnished with Parsley)—Quail on Toast.
Scalloped Oysters.
Salad Egg—Celery—Stuffed Tomatoes.
English Plum Pudding (Wine Sauce).
Chocolate Cream—Vanilla Cream.
Orange Ice.
Fancy Cake—Chocolate.

SUMMER LUNCH.

Mock Bisquit.
Cold Sliced Tongue—Jellied Chicken.
Lobster Croquettes.
Pickled Shad—Sardines (with Lemon Pigs).
Sliced Tomatoes—Lettuce.
Sponge Pudding—Lemon Pie.
Ice Cream—Frozen Peaches.
Fancy Cake—Coffee.

Cut a slit underneath one end of a lemon; this represents the snout of a pig, two small cloves above for eyes, four matches for feet; hold over sardines, squeeze the sides of lemon, the juice will ooze from mouth.

SMALL EVENING COMPANY.

Pickled Oysters.
Lobster Salad—Chicken Salad.
Ham Sandwiches—Tongue Sandwiches.
Fruit—Creams—Ices.
Jelly—Cake.
Coffee—Lemonade.

LARGE EVENING COMPANY.

OYSTERS.
Stewed—Pickled—Fried.
Ham Sandwiches—Tongue Sandwiches.—Chicken Sandwiches.
Boned Turkey—Chicken Salad—Lobster Salad.
Charlotte Russe—Wine Jelly.
Creams (in shapes of small birds).
Creams and Ices, in forms of Bricks.
Fancy Cakes—Bananas—Grapes—Oranges.
Coffee—Lemonade.

The Leading

CLOTHIERS.

Boys' Clothing

A SPECIALTY.

402 & 404 FULTON ST., cor. Gallatin Place, Brooklyn.

487 BROADWAY, cor. Broome Street, New York.

E. R. Durkee & Co.'s Salad Dressing.

This is universally pronounced in the clubs, by connoisseurs and all who have used it, the most delicious mayonaise dressing ever put on the market. It is adapted to every variety of meat and vegetable salads, to raw tomatoes, cabbage, pickled salmon, cold meats, &c , &c. It is prepared with extreme care ; all its ingredients are of the *purest* and *best*. It is cheaper than home-made dressings, and will keep good for years.

E. R. Durkee & Co 's Select Spices.
With Trade-mark of the Gauntlet.

Under this brand we put up, in tin cans of various sizes, *absolutely* pure Spices, which, being ground from the very choicest varieties, cannot possibly be excelled in strength or flavor. Those who want *pure* and *fine-flavored* spices should buy our brand of Select Spices. They are the cheapest, and will prove to be by far the most satisfactory. To avoid deception, buy them *only* in unopened cans or packets, and see that our trade-mark of the gauntlet and signature is on the labels.

E. R. Durkee & Co.'s Baking Powder.

The analysis of this article by a United States Government chemist, in 1876 and 1877, showed that it contained a larger per centum of carbonic acid gas, and consequently greater leavening power, than any other powder presented for examination. It was pronounced, in all essentials, the *best*, and the Government ordered it in preference to any other. In ¼, ½, and 1 lb. full-weight cans.

E. R. Durkee & Co.'s Flavoring Extracts.

Made from selected materials and with the greatest possible care to preserve the true fruit flavor, that they may really take the place of the fruit for which they are substituted. They are of great strength—a single teaspoonful being equal to half a bottle of some kinds. They contain no poisonous oils or acids, are perfectly pure, and uniform in quality.

E. R. Durkee & Co.'s Pastry Spice.

A combination of Spices for pies, custard, puddings, sweet sauces, hot drinks, &c.; designed for those who either find it difficult to get the right proportions when several Spices are used, or inconvenient to keep on hand all those most suitable for the purpose.

E. R. Durkee & Co.'s Golden Starch.
For Dark Prints, Mourning Goods, etc.

Common laundry starch is *insoluble* in water, and it is well known that when very dark goods are starched with it they have a soiled and dirty appearance, and never look as well as at first. The Golden Starch is perfectly *soluble* in cold or hot water, and the darkest goods—even crape—when starched with it, *look as bright and clear as when new*. With it almost any desired degree of stiffness may be given to goods, and they will retain their stiffness much longer than when common starch is used.

E. R. Durkee & Co.'s Laundry Blue.

In powder, in pepper-box style. The intense coloring power of this bluing, its ready solubility in hard or soft water, the low price at which it is sold, its neat and convenient shape, make it the cheapest and most desirable of all bluings.

E. R. Durkee & Co.'s Sewing Machine Oil.

Under our trade-mark of the gauntlet, we put up an oil refined and prepared from the best lubricator known, expressly for the purpose ; it never corrodes, gums, or rusts, and will far outwear the oils usally sold.

E. R. DURKEE & CO.'S Manufactures

Are sold nearly everywhere by dealers most particular in the quality of their goods. If your grocer cannot supply you, go elsewhere for them.

PRINCIPAL OFFICE, 135, 137 & 139. WATER STREET, NEW YORK.

DURYEAS'
IMPROVED CORN STARCH,

Is an entirely pure and delicate preparation, from the best varieties of Maize. It affords many delicate and nourishing dishes. The process of its manufacture is the latest and most improved.

DURYEAS'
Satin Gloss Starch,

IN SIX-POUND BOXES AND ONE-POUND PAPERS.

Try it. Gives a beautiful white and glossy finish, besides renders fabrics very durable. No other Starch so easily used, or so economical.

Use it Once and You Will Use no Other.

DURYEAS' STARCH,

In every instance of competition, has received the highest award.

In addition to Medals many Diplomas have been received. The following are a few of the characterizing terms of award:

At London, 1862, for quality   "EXCEEDINGLY EXCELLENT."
" Paris, 1867, for   "PERFECTION OF PREPARATION."
" Centennial, 1876, for   "NOTABLE OR ABSOLUTE PURITY."
Franklin Institute, Penn.,   "FOR BEING THE BEST
KNOWN TO EXIST IN THE MARKET OF AMERICAN PRODUCTION."

FOR SALE BY GROCERS GENERALLY.

Be Sure "DURYEAS'" is on Every Package.

Our new Recipe Book will be sent post-paid to any one sending us their address.

General Depot, 29, 31 and 33 Park Place, New York.

BORDEN'S
CONDENSED MILK

Is applicable to all purposes for which other fresh milk is used, and for many purposes is superior.

Four parts of water to one part Condensed Milk makes richer milk than the fluid milk ordinarily sold.

Condensed to the standard suited to city use, it will remain sweet two or three times as long as common milk, *with the same care*.

THE COMPANY CLAIMS THAT IT GIVES MORE REAL MILK FOR THE SAME AMOUNT OF MONEY THAN IS SOLD IN NEW YORK, BROOKLYN OR VICINITY.

As a healthful diet for Infants and Children, hundreds of the patrons of this Company have testified.

Borden's Preserved Milk,
GAIL BORDEN EAGLE BRAND.

BORDEN'S EXTRACT OF COFFEE.
Prepared from the finest grades of coffee, combined with refined sugar and Borden's Condensed Milk.

BORDEN'S PURE COCOA,
In combination with Borden's Condensed Milk and Refined Sugar.

Office, 98, 100, 102, 104 & 106 Sterling Place,
BROOKLYN.

The Excelsior Wringer,
FOR STATIONARY TUBS.

This Wringer possesses all the excellencies of any round tub machine, and in addition has a Patent Reversible Water Board for conducting the water into either division of the stationary tub desired, thus saving the time and labor of changing the Wringer from one partition of the tub to the other—a very important advantage, which belongs *exclusively* to the "Excelsior."

Please send for an illustrated circular and price list to

BAILEY WRINGING MACHINE CO.,

99 Chambers St., New York.

HECKERS' SUPERLATIVE SELF-RAISING FLOUR,

Is constantly becoming more popular with those willing to pay for an article that will make the finest bread ever put upon a table, with unfailing certainty, if the few simple directions for baking be properly observed.

Heckers' Farina.

A delicious article of food, a beautiful ornament for the table, it is very agreeable, light and nutritious. A superior article for puddings and jellies.

Of Special Importance.

Heckers' Self-Raising Griddle Cake Flour.

Although it is only three years since this article was introduced to the public it has become as popular as the other well-known brands of HECKER'S SELF-RAISING FLOUR, which have been so extensively used for making Bread, Biscuit, Cakes, etc., for the past twenty-seven years.

It is decidedly the cheapest and best preparation known for making Griddle Cakes, Wheat Cakes, or Pan Cakes, Muffins, Fritters, etc., producing at a moment's notice, by the addition only of cold water or milk, most delicious, light and wholesome Cakes, which, unlike those made with yeast, may be eaten while hot without detriment.

* The Griddle Cake Flour is used by many in preference to Buckwheat.

RECIPE FOR GRIDDLE CAKES.—One and a half pounds of the Griddle Cake Flour, one pint of cold milk, and one pint of cold water—or all water may be used. Have the griddle hot before you mix the batter. Mix the flour with two-thirds of the liquor, stir thoroughly, then add the balance. This is sufficient for about thirty-five ordinary sized Cakes.

Put up for the convenience of families, hotels and restaurants, in 3 and 6 lb. packages, 24 ½ lb. bags, barrels and half barrels, with all directions for use.

HECKERS' SELF-RAISING BUCKWHEAT,

Will be found decidedly the cheapest, when the saving of time and trouble is considered. It is always ready, always reliable, and perfectly healthy. Dyspeptics and persons that cannot eat Buckwheat Cakes made by the old process with yeast, can use the Self-Raising Buckwheat without detriment.

No more "mixing Buckwheat over night," but in the morning, when the griddle is hot, to 3 pounds of

Heckers' Self-Raising Buckwheat,

add 5 pints of water or milk, or part each, and bake immediately. Keep the batter in a cool place if not wanted for immediate use. This will produce seventy light and delicious Cakes, preferred by many to those made with yeast.

Put up for the convenience of families, hotels and restaurants, in 3 and 6 lb. packages, 24 ¼ lb. bags, barrels, half barrels, with full directions for use.

GEO. V. HECKER & CO.
CROTON MILLS,
203 CHERRY ST., NEW YORK.

REDHEAD'S Baking Powder.

For over fifteen years **Redhead's Baking Powder** has been before the Brooklyn public, and has met with a continually increasing demand. Its superior quality gained for it a prize medal in competition with others, and its general excellence has merited a preference from all who have used it, as may be seen by the following gratuitous notice:

"**Redhead's Baking Powder** has attained an extensive sale in some sections of Brooklyn, and many people would have no other."—*Housekeeper's Companion.* Editor's answer to the question, "Who makes the best Baking Powder?"

ASK YOUR GROCER FOR IT.

Manufactory, 280 Pearl Street, New York.

The Fulton Ave. Tea Market.

WM. S. CARLISLE,

Wholesale and Retail

Tea and Coffee Dealer and General Grocer,

493 FULTON ST., BROOKLYN, N. Y.

Specialties: Teas, Coffees, Sugars and Flour.

CATALOGUES MAILED FREE ON APPLICATION.

Goods delivered to any part of the City or Wharves or Railroad Depots in New York or Brooklyn, free of charge.

GOLDEN ANCHOR
HOUSE FURNISHING EMPORIUM,
SAMUEL B. MASSA.

China, Glass, Cutlery,
WOODEN AND TIN WARES.
Children's Carriages.

991 & 993 Fulton Street, Brooklyn.

LANG & NAU.
Artistic Furniture,
FROM MEDIÆVAL DESIGNS.

Interior Decorations.

HARDWOOD MANTLES, PIER AND MANTLE MIRRORS.

294 Fulton Street, Brooklyn, N. Y.

CHARLES M. JACOBSON,

Manufacturer,

425 Fulton St., (near Pearl) BROOKLYN.

FINE DRESS HATS FOR GENTLEMEN.

Derby Hats, Soft Felt Hats, Opera Hats,
Traveling Hats and Caps,

AT POPULAR PRICES.

HATS FOR YOUTHS, BOYS and CHILDREN.

The Latest Styles. Fine Hats for Dress.

Durable Hats for School, &c., &c.

LOCKITT'S
GOLDEN CANISTER TEA WAREHOUSES,

Established 1852.

Wholesale and Retail Dealers in

Teas, Coffees & Fancy Groceries,

FULTON STREET, COR. ORANGE,	185 MYRTLE AVENUE,
559 FULTON STREET,	DE KALB AVE. COR. NOSTRAND,
14, 16 & 18 DE KALB AVENUE,	89 ATLANTIC AVENUE.

BROOKLYN.

RANDEL, BAREMORE & CO.

DIAMONDS

Cor. Maiden Lane & Nassau St.,

No. 29 MAIDEN LANE,   *NEW YORK.*
& 58 NASSAU STREET,

No. 51A CONDUIT STREET,   *LONDON, W.*

CHAS. B. YALE.   G. SELDEN YALE.

SIMPSON, HALL, MILLER & CO.,

Manufacturers of the Finest Quality

SILVER PLATED WARES

676 BROADWAY,

Factories, Wallingford, Conn.   NEW YORK.

HOWARD
FIRE INSURANCE CO.

Of NEW YORK.

CHARTERED 1825.

Cash Capital, ... $500,000.

OFFICE, 66 WALL STREET, NEW YORK.

SAMUEL T. SKIDMORE, Prest. HENRY A. OAKLEY, Vice-Prest.
CHARLES A. HULL, Sec'y. RICHARD W. CLARK, Asst. Sec'y.

DAISY CREAM.

N. Y. P. O. Box 4589.  For Sale by first-class Druggists.

Certain and Harmless Cure for all Skin Diseases.

THE FOLLOWING FROM A BROOKLYN LADY.

Brooklyn, Jan. 21st, 1877.

For the sake of benefiting others, I consent to give my testimony in regard to "Daisy Cream." A physician of well acknowledged standing advised me to use your lotion,—he having known of several cases that had been cured by its use, other means having failed. At his suggestion, I bought it, and a few bottles have made my complexion perfectly clear. My entire face had been covered with a most repulsive eruption, my health was seriously affected, and great expense had been incurred for physicians' fees, amounting to hundreds of dollars. The irritating cause having been removed, my health is restored.

JOURNEAY & BURNHAM,

DRY GOODS,

126 & 128 ATLANTIC ST,

BROOKLYN.

C. M. WEST,

Successor to DICKENSON & WEST.

251 & 253 Fulton Street,

BROOKLYN.

DRY GOODS

AT POPULAR PRICES.

Goods marked down. Black Silks at astonishingly low prices. One invoice Guinet's Black Silks at $1.25 per yard—a great bargain. Headquarters for Black Cashmeres. Mourning Goods a specialty.

J. GILDERSLEEVE,

DEALER IN

FISH, OYSTERS, CLAMS, LOBSTERS, &c.

354 Fulton St., cor. Red Hook Lane,

BROOKLYN.

A. & E. ROBBINS,

DEALERS IN

POULTRY & GAME

of all kinds,

Nos. 125 & 127 FULTON COUNTRY MARKET,

NEW YORK.

N. B.—Ships and Parties supplied at the shortest notice.

STANDARD
FIRE INSURANCE COMPANY.

Office, 62 Liberty Street,

NEW YORK.

Insurance Against Fire.

SAFETY FUND POLICIES ISSUED.

WM. M. ST. JOHN,   WILLIAM CRIPPS,
Vice-Pres't & Sec'y.   President.

LAMAR
Insurance Co. of New York,
BROADWAY, cor. JOHN ST.

Capital, - - - - $200,000.

ASSETS, JANUARY 1st, 1878.

Cash on hand and in Bank,	$ 16,660.07
United States Bonds, market value,	268,700.00
Loans on Call, Good Stocks Collateral,	9,300.00
Bonds and Mortgages on Brick Dwellings,	77,400.00
Bills Receivable for Inland Premiums,	835.00
Premiums in course of collection,	10,890.06
New York Bank Stocks, market value,	15,120.00
	$398,805.13

Liabilities, including Re-Insurance,	$71,886.01
Surplus over Capital and Liabilities,	$126,919.12

ISAAC R. ST. JOHN, Pres't.   **A. R. FROTHINGHAM, Vice-Pres't.**
WM. R. MACDIARMID, Sec'y.

Baker & Clark's
PREMIUM HAM,
THE WORLD'S BEST.

This HAM excels all others. Cured with Granulated Sugar. Mild and of Delicious Flavor. Carefully Selected. Are put up in Attractive Style.

These HAMS are recommended to every family as the choicest in the market. Address,

BAKER & CLARK,
335 & 337 Greenwich St., N. Y.

AUSTEN'S
Oswego Baking Powder.

Warranted strictly pure and healthy. Keeps good in any climate. Once tried always used. Full weight exclusive of can. Triple strength. Is invaluable where economy, health, and delicious cooking are appreciated. It is perfectly white and pure. Manufactured by an entirely new process, and is as much superior to Baking Powder made after the old process as patent new process flours are to those made the old way. It is not subject to atmospheric influences; will not lose its strength or become lumpy; and when used according to directions, most satisfactory results are sure to follow. For sale by all first-class grocers.

BAKER & CLARK, Agents,
NEW YORK.

Hazelton Brothers,
Manufacturers of

GRAND, SQUARE & UPRIGHT
PIANO-FORTES.

These Pianos have always received the First Premium whe.ever they have been exhibited, for

Elast'c Touch, Singing Quality, Delicacy and Power of Tone.

GREAT DURABILITY.

WAREROOMS:

34 & 36 University Place, bet. 10th & 11th Sts.,

NEW YORK.

A. J. MEAGHER,
UPHOLSTERER,

96 Orange St., near Fulton St., Brooklyn.

Gold Band and Holland Shades and Fixtures,

IN EVERY VARIETY, MADE TO ORDER, AT LOWEST PRICES.

HAIR, HUSK, STRAW and SPRING BEDS.

Moss, Tow, Excelsior and other MATTRESSES.

FEATHERS.

LACE CURTAINS cleaned equal to new. OLD MATTRESSES re-picked and made over equal to new. CARPETS re-fitted and laid, all at the MOST MODERATE PRICES.

CROSSMAN & BERGEN,

Best Fitting, Best Wearing,

LOWEST PRICE,

FINE BOOTS & SHOES.

Complete Assortment for

Gents, Boys, Ladies, Misses and Children,

599 FULTON STREET,

Opposite Flatbush Ave.,   *BROOKLYN.*

HEALTH FOOD COMPANY,

Established 1874.

INTRODUCERS OF

Perfect Assimilative Food,

FOR THE

Preservation of Health & the Alleviation & Cure of Disease,

Through the agency of simple and unmysterious preparations of

Wheat, Barley, Oats, Rye, Corn, Fruit, Meats, etc.

Manufactured by new and superior processes, freed from all objectionable admixtures, and containing all those essential food constituents demanded for the relief of Disorders of the Digestive, Nervous, Biliary, Urinary and Circulatory Systems that are now so prevalent and fatal in this country, the natural results of excessive mental and physical labor, accompanied by an unpardonable ignorance or carelessness in reference to all Hygienic principles.

Brooklyn Office, No. 9 Clinton St., Brooklyn, N. Y.

CIRCULARS FREE.

HOME OFFICE, 74 FOURTH AVE., NEW YORK CITY.

S. O. BURNETT,

DEALER IN

HARDWARE,

House-Furnishing Goods,

FANCY BASKETS, &c.,

No. 288 FULTON STREET,

BROOKLYN.

NEW LESTER SAW.

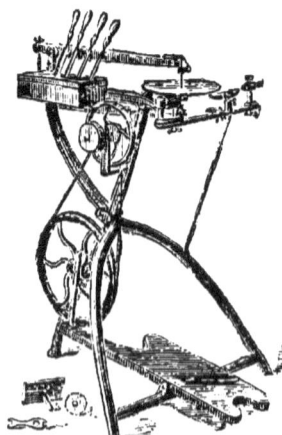

It consists of, first, a SCROLL-SAW, with Tilting-Table for inlaid work; arms 18 inches in the clear; clamps which will hold saws of any length or width, and face them in four different directions; cutting lumber from one-sixteenth to one inch in thickness; speed, 1,000 strokes per minute.

Second, a CIRCULAR SAW, two and one-half inches in diameter, which will cut lumber one-half inch and less; with an iron table, four by five inches.

Third, a DRILLING ATTACHMENT, with six Stubs' Steel Drills, of various sizes, for wood or iron work.

Fourth, an EMERY WHEEL, with wide and narrow rim.

Fifth, a TURNING-LATHE, with iron ways and rest, steel centres, and three best steel turning tools; length of ways, 15 inches; distance between centres, 9 inches; swing, 3 inches; length of slide-rest, 4½ inches; number of revolutions per minute, 7,000.

Also, with each machine, six Saw-blades, a Wrench, Screw-driver, extra Belt, and two sheets of Designs, with a nice box for the small tools, and a box for the whole machine. It is taken apart when shipped, and packed in a box, but the working parts are all left in place, and the frame is put together again by a single bolt.

Price for every thing above named, $8; the same, without the lathe and circular saw, $6.

When desired, we furnish with the Lathe a very nice Drill-Chuck, for working metal, and a Tail Stock, with a screw centre, for $2 extra.

MILLERS FALLS CO., 74 Chambers St., N. Y.

SHELDON & WADSWORTH,

BANKERS AND BROKERS,

No. 10 WALL STREET,

Will give careful attention to the Purchase and Sale of

STOCKS, BONDS OR GOLD,

on commission, making advances on same when desired.

EDWARD MILLER & CO.

BRONZES,

No. 35 WARREN STREET,

Cor. Church Street,

NEW YORK.

PAINT WORKS: Horatio and Jane Streets, New York.

ARTISTS' MATERIALS.
F. W. DEVOE & CO.,
Cor. Fulton and William sts., New York,
MANUFACTURERS OF
ARTISTS' OIL COLORS, IN TUBES;
CANVAS, ACADEMY BOARDS, MILLBOARDS, AND OIL-SKETCHING PAPERS;
Fine Brushes for Oil and Water Color Painting.
VARNISHES, WATER COLOR LIQUIDS, OILS, ETC.
Drawing Papers, Sketching Books and Blocks, Pencils, Mathematical Instruments,

Charcoal and Crayon Drawing Materials,
Illustrated Books on Art, Folding and Studio Easels, Drawing Boards, Studies, Manikins and Lay-Figures, Out-of-door Sketching Boxes.
WINSOR & NEWTON'S
CAKE AND MOIST WATER COLORS,
Tube Colors, Canvas, etc.; also, French and German Goods.
SCULPTORS' TOOLS, MODELING WAX AND CLAY.
PLASTER CASTS FOR MODELS.
ANTIQUE POTTERY AND PORCELAIN TILES, with materials for Pottery and China Decoration.
Fresco Designs and Colors, and Brushes for Fresco and Scenic Painting.
WAX FLOWER SUPPLIES: COLORS, TOOLS, MOULDS AND BRUSHES.
Manufacturers of WHITE LEAD, ZINC WHITE, COLORS and VARNISHES.
Factories—Horatio and Jane streets.

FRED'K W. DEVOE,   JAMES F. DRUMMOND.   FRED'K SAUNDERS, JR.,   J. SEAVER P

These Goods for Sale by
THOS. HANSON, 98 Myrtle Ave., Brooklyn.

PRIZE MEDAL, PARIS MARITIME EXHIBITION, 1875.

NEAVE'S FOOD

FOR

INFANTS AND INVALIDS.

Is pre-eminently rich in albumenoids and phosphates, and the starch which it contains is in a state readily assimilated by the infantile digestion. This desirable result is obtained by a judicious selection of farinas, and by very careful manipulation in the process of cooking.

Neave's Food has received the high and unqualified approval of eminent medical men for many years past. Amongst those who recommend it are: Drs. Cameron, M. P., Hassall, Barker, Bartlett, etc., etc., and the late eminent Drs. Lankester, Ruddock, and Letheby.

Neave's Food commands a ready sale where once introduced, for it is strongly recommended by mothers to the notice of their lady friends; and infants often give it a preference, refusing other foods. As a natural result the sale has extended rapidly, especially during the past three years, necessitating the erection of extensive premises, where the preparation is carried on under the personal supervision of Mr. Neave.

Neave's Food is sent in large quantities to the Colonies and to the United States. It is prepared with special reference to exportation.

Neave's Food is sold in tins and tinfoil packets, by chemists and storekeepers at home and abroad.

For terms, apply to any wholesale or export house, or to the manufacturers,

JOSIAH R. NEAVE & CO.,
Fordingbridge, England.

AGENT FOR THE STATES,

J. O. NOXON,
444 Fulton Street, Brooklyn, N. Y.

EARL'S BOARDING AND LIVERY STABLES,
No. 80 IRVING PLACE, near Fulton St., Brooklyn, N. Y.

Particlar Attention Paid to Grooming. Clarences and Coaches To Let at All Hours. Wedding, Shopping and Visiting Calls Promptly Attended To.

C. E. EARL, Proprietor.

BRANCH OFFICE—No. 8 Putnam Ave., near Fulton-St.

CHAS. E. EARL,
FURNISHING UNDERTAKER,

3 PUTNAM AVE., opp. Fulton Street.

FUNERALS ATTENDED TO IN FIRST-CLASS ORDER.

SEXTON of Dr. Duryea's Classon Ave. Presbyterian Church.

THE LIGHT RUNNING "DOMESTIC" SEWING MACHINE

Possesses all the excellencies of all other Sewing Machines, without their defects. It makes the best stitch, is most readily operated, has the widest range of work, does not fatigue, and is almost noiseless. Home Office, Broadway and 14th Street, New York.

THE EVER RELIABLE "DOMESTIC" PAPER FASHIONS

Retain their popularity and reputation as the BEST of patterns for ladies' wear. The styles are the most recent and elegant, and the excellent system by which they are cut insures a perfectly fitting garment.

The Most Remarkable curative remedies ever given to the public are the Centaur Liniments. They have already acquired a sale greater than that of any other Liniment, Ointment, Extract, Pain-Killer, Embrocation or Salve. A list of the ingredients accompanying each bottle. A pamphlet containing a history of the Centaurs, the discovery of these recipes, and several hundred testimonials of the marvelous results of the Liniments, from well-known physicians and public men, will be sent upon application. The Centaur Liniments are of two kinds: the White is for family use, delicate and pleasant; the Yellow is for horses and animals. They always subdue swellings and alleviate pain. They heal scalds and burns without a scar. They cure Rheumatism, Neuralgia, Sciatica, Strains, Sprains, Stiff Joints, Bruises, Ulcers, Nervous Headache, Caked Breasts, Sore Nipples, etc. The White Liniment exterminates Pimples and removes Freckles. It extracts the poison from the stings and bites of insects and reptiles. As an external remedy for Bronchitis, Sore Throat, Quinsey, Croup and Mumps, its effects have never been equaled. The Yellow Centaur Liniment is a certain, quick and cheap remedy for Spavin, Sweeny, Scratches, Strains, Wounds, etc., upon horses and other animals. It is absolute death to Screw-Worms in sheep. It is worth its weight in gold to planters, farmers, liverymen and owners of animals. The Centaur Liniments are sold for 50 cents and $1.00, by every druggist in America. Full directions are around each bottle. The fifty cent and dollar bottles contain three times and eight times the quantity of the 25 cent trial bottles. Address

THE CENTAUR COMPANY, 46 Dey Street, New York.

Castoria, a substitute for Castor Oil, after the recipe of Dr. Samuel Pitcher, Hyannis, Mass., is the only preparation for babies and children suffering from Wind Colic, Stomach Ache, Teething, Loss of Sleep, Worms, etc., which does not contain Morphine or some kind of narcotic drug. Pitcher's Castoria neither gripes nor gags. It is as pleasant to take as honey, and is as harmless as farina. It assimilates the food in the stomach, and by causing natural digestion and evacuation, affords quiet to the child, and rest to the mother. It is warranted to contain neither mineral, morphine nor alcohol. The price is 35 cents, in large bottles, covered by full directions. It is sold by all druggists everywhere.

AVILA & BARKER,

Decorators,

PAINTERS AND PAPER HANGERS,

145 Fulton Street,

JOHN AVILA,
WM. G. BARKER.

BROOKLYN.

Window Shades.

STEWART & CO.,

Importers and Dealers in

CARPETING,

Oil Cloth & Upholstery Goods,

174 FULTON, AND 53, 55 & 57 HENRY STS.,

BROOKLYN.

———◆———

Druggets, Mattings, Rugs, Stair Rods, Shades, Mattresses, &c., &c.

FURNITURE TAKEN ON STORAGE.

S. B. STEWART.   L. V. D. HARDENBERGH.

HULL'S
CONCAVE CAST-IRON GALVANIZED
CHIMNEY TOP AND VENTILATOR,
Warranted to Cure Smoky Chimneys.
NO CURE! NO PAY!

We offer our new Cast-Iron Chimney Top and Ventilator to the public, as the Cheapest, most Efficient, Durable and Ornamental Ventilator yet Invented, and claim for it advantages over all others,

AS FOLLOWS:

1st. It is made entirely of Cast-Iron, and Galvanized.
2nd. Costs less than a Sheet-Iron Top and Base.
3rd. Durability guaranteed.
4th. Forms, unlike all others, its own base, saving time and expense.
5th. A flue may vary from 8x8 to 12x12 in. and the same top will fit.
6th. Is an ornament to any building.
7th. If painted and sanded resembles a heavy brown stone cap.
8th. No rain or moisture can enter the flue.
9th. Is so constructed that outside currents of air increase the draft.
10th. No downward drafts possible.
11th. Protects the brick-work of the chimney.
12th. The top of the Ventilator is easily removed to clean the flue.
13th. Are made to cover from one to five flues, under one top.
14th. When one flue is in use the top is heated, which increases the draft of all.
15th. As a Ventilator for Churches, Hotels, Schools, Breweries, Factories and Private Houses they are unsurpassed.

The Following is Offered as a Sample Reference:

MR. M. C. HULL.   100 Fourth Avenue, New York, Sept. 19th, 1877.
Dear Sir:—The success of your Patent Cast-Iron Chimney Top now in use on my house, No. 316 Madison Avenue, is all that can be desired. I have tried several other kinds all to no purpose, and I am agreeably surprised to find your Patent Top a success. Please put fourteen more on same house, enough to cover every flue, at your earliest convenience, and oblige,

Yours, very respectfully,   MALTBY G. LANE.

DAYTON & CARTER,
Fulton Street, near Flatbush Avenue, Brooklyn,
AGENTS FOR LONG ISLAND.

New Store.
PORTER & THORBURN,
372 & 374 Fulton Street, Brooklyn,
ARE SELLING

YARD.	YARD.
Best White Piques....... 5¾c.	Bl'k F'ch Cashmeres 50c. worth 75c.
Best Standard Prints.... 4½c.	2-But. Lisle Thr'd Gloves,25c." 50c.
Beautiful Colored Hilla...... 7¾c.	3 But. " " " 30c." 65c.
Ex. Cashmere Silks (Blk.),$1.00	4-But. " " " 35c." 70c.
Colored Cashmeres .... 14¾c.	

PORTER & THORBURN.

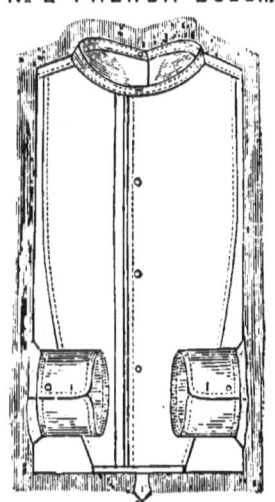

Nº 2 FRENCH BOSOM.

Sign of the D Gold Shirt.

ITHAMAR DU BOIS,

328 Fulton Street, Brooklyn,

FINE

𝕾hirt 𝕸aker

AND

Men's Furnisher.

JOSEPH O'BRIEN & CO.

Importers, Manufacturers and Dealers in

DRY GOODS

Carpets, Clothing,

141 & 143, 151 to 159 ATLANTIC AVE.,

BROOKLYN.

JOSEPH O'BRIEN,
JULIUS MEYER,
W. E. CAPEN.

W. S. LISTER,

DEALER IN

Beef, Mutton, Lamb & Veal,

11 & 13 CONCORD STREET,

NEAR FULTON STREET,   BROOKLYN.

FISH, OYSTERS, VEGETABLES AND GAME,

IN SEASON.

Every article warranted of the choicest quality.

MARKETING SENT TO ALL PARTS OF THE CITY.

F. W. PFANNKUCHEN,

Wholesale and Retail Dealer in

Foreign and Domestic Fruits,

238 & 242 FULTON ST.,

Cor. Clark,   BROOKLYN.

FAMILY FLOUR.

S. VALENTINE'S SONS,

169 & 171 Cherry St.,

Established 1822.   COR. MARKET SLIP,

NEW YORK.

Flour delivered in any part of Brooklyn or New York City free of charge. Special attention given to selecting the choicest qualities for family use.

C. MOLLENHAGEN,

CONFECTIONERY

AND

Fancy Cake Bakery,

ICE CREAM AND ICES,

Fancy Cream, Charlotte Russe, Jellies, Pyramids, etc.,

No. 197 ATLANTIC AVENUE,

Between Court and Clinton Streets,   **BROOKLYN.**

All orders attended to at shortest notice.

T. BROOKS & CO.'S SUCCESSORS,

Furniture & Decorations,

137, 139, 141 & 143 FULTON ST.,

BROOKLYN.

F. A. BALDWIN.   E. PEARCE TAYLOR.   WM. A. DAVIS.

GEDNEY & NUNGASSER,
HOUSE FURNISHING GOODS.

212 & 214 FULTON ST., COR. PINEAPPLE ST.,
BROOKLYN.
China, Crockery, Glassware, Lamps, &c., &c.

JAMES ARMSTRONG,

Of the late firm

ARMSTRONG & BLACKLIN,

Plumber & Gas-Fitter,

349 COURT STREET, near Union,

BROOKLYN.

Having had twenty-three years' experience in all branches of the trade, offers his services to householders and builders.

SANITARY PLUMBING A SPECIALTY.

ANDERSON'S
CONFECTIONERY

AND

LADIES' SALOON,

Cor. Fulton & Clinton Streets, Brooklyn.

Wedding, Dinner, and Evening Parties furnished entire with Silver, China, Bridal and Fancy Cakes; also, Ice Cream, Ices, Charlotte de Russe, Jelly, etc., in every variety.

SALOON
Open Until Midnight.

ASK YOUR GROCER FOR

HIGGINS' GERMAN LAUNDRY SOAP

THE BEST IN USE.

ACKER, MERRALL & CONDIT,

IMPORTERS OF

Fine Wines and Havana Cigars,

DEALERS IN

FINE GROCERIES,

Nos. 130 & 132 CHAMBERS ST.,

And Cor. Broadway and 42d St.,

NEW YORK.

39 RUE DE LAFAYETTE, PARIS.

1840.   Thirty-eight Years Experience.   1878.

JOSEPH G. UNDERHILL,
DRUGGIST,
CLASSON, COR. OF GREENE AVENUE, BROOKLYN.

Only Articles of FIRST QUALITY Sold or Dispensed.

PHYSICIANS' PRESCRIPTIONS AND FAMILY RECIPES A SPECIALTY.

A Great Variety of Goods pertaining to the Toilet and Nursery.

Fine French, English and German Perfumery, Pomades,

HAIR OILS, TOILET POWDER, &c.,

TOOTH, HAIR, NAIL AND FLESH BRUSHES,
DRESSING AND IVORY FINE COMBS AND RUBBER GOODS,
WHITMAN'S FINE CONFECTIONERY.

The Purest and Best Foreign Brandies and Wines.

Bourbon and other Whiskies, California and other native Wines, Scotch Ale, London Porter, Natural and Artificial Mineral Waters of all kinds, in Siphons and Bottles. Sparkling and Cold Soda Water, with Choice Fruit and Cream Syrups.

HOMŒOPATHIC BOOKS AND MEDICINES,
TINCTURES, TRITURATIONS, SUGAR OF MILK, PELLETS, DILUTIONS, &c.

Also, "Humphreys' Homeopathic Specifics" and Witch-Hazel.

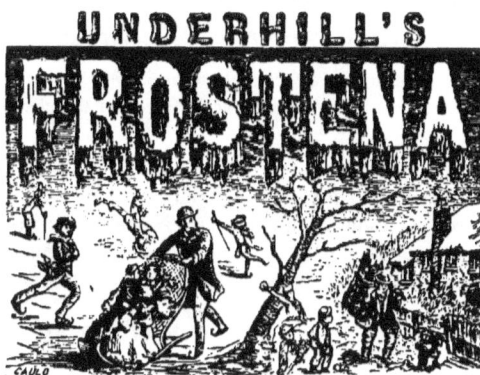

FOR CHAPPED HANDS, FACE, AND LIPS.

FROSTENA is most deliciously perfumed, contains no oil or grease, and will not soil the clothes. FROSTENA makes the face and hands soft. Gentlemen should use it after shaving. FROSTENA *removes Tan and Sunburn.*

ECKLER, Printer, 35 Fulton St., N. Y.

SILVER WHITING.

TRADE MARK.

For Cleaning and Polishing

Gold AND Silver,
Silver Plated & Nickel Plated Ware.

Prepared expressly for and Warranted Pure by

JOSEPH G. UNDERHILL,
BROOKLYN, N. Y.

In offering this article to the public, I do not claim it to be a new discovery, but simply what it is represented to be, viz :

A PURE SILVER WHITING,

free from grit or any impurity and capable of imparting a finer, more brilliant and permanent lustre, than any article ever offered for the cleaning of Silver or Plated Ware.

The vast superiority of a pure quality of Silver Whiting over all other preparations in the market for cleaning and polishing Silver and Plated goods has always been known; but in many instances the public has been induced by high sounding or foreign names to use chemically prepared POISONOUS COMPOUNDS, unfit, to say the least, if not dangerous for family use.

PRICE, 10 CENTS A PACKAGE.

SILVER WHITING will be found superior to Soap for Cleaning all kinds of Glassware.

MRS. DISBROW'S

A Soothing Cordial for
Infants and Children Teething.

A safe and pleasant-medicine for infants and children teething, and for all diseases incident to the infantile system; and is a SPEEDY CURE FOR CHOLIC, CRAMPS, AND WINDY PAINS. It is of excellent use to children that are of a restless and fretful habit; and to those who are greatly troubled with GRIPING, VOMITING, OR LOOSENESS, a few doses of the cordial will give immediate ease. CHILDREN CUTTING THEIR TEETH HARD, and thereby suffering intense pain, may be considerably relieved by applying a small portion of the ANISETT to the finger, and rubbing the gums gently for a short time. The collection of wind in the stomach often causes and gives rise to the most intense and excruciating pain, which a timely dose of the ANISETT will remove almost immediately.

Mothers! this ANISETT will give you rest and make your children cheerful and happy. Don't let them cry for the want of it.

RETAILED BY
DRUGGISTS EVERYWHERE.
Price, Twenty-five Cents.

Sulphate of Iron,
(COPPERAS.)

For use as a disinfectant, dissolve one pound in a gallon of water. A pint of solution should be poured into the water-closet pans night and morning.

In Packages with full Directions.

PRICE, 10 CENTS.

QUILLAY,
OR
SOAP TREE BARK.

This BARK is well adapted to the cleansing of soiled Silks and other fabrics, the colors or gloss of which are destroyed by soaps. It is also much used in the tropics as a wash for the hair and skin.

In Packages with full Directions.

PRICE, 10 CENTS.

UNDERHILL'S
FROSTENA
SOAP.

The Cosmetic qualities of this exquisite Soap are such, that by its constant use not only are chaps prevented, but all roughness and excoriations of the Skin are entirely removed, rendering it an indispensable requisite to the toilet of Ladies, and those of tender skin.

☞ MOTHERS SHOULD USE IT FOR THEIR INFANTS. ☜

THE ONLY CHEMICALLY PURE BORAX OFFERED FOR SALE.

It may be useful to some of our readers to learn that refined borax is now generally substituted for soda, as a washing powder, in the proportion of a large handful to about ten gallons of boiling water; thus saving half the usual quantity of soap employed. All large washing establishments adopt this method, and it is used extensively in Holland and Belgium, where the laundresses are famous for the beautiful whiteness of their linen. For laces and cambrics an extra quantity of the powder is used, and for crinolines (required to be made very stiff) a strong solution is necessary. Borax being a neutral salt does not in the slightest degree injure the linen; its effect is to soften the hardest water; and, therefore, it should be kept on every toilette table. To the taste it is rather sweet, is used for cleansing the hair, is an excellent dentrifice, and in hot countries is used in combination with tartaric acid and bicarbonate of soda, as a cooling beverage. Good tea cannot be made with hard water; all water may be made soft by adding a teaspoonful of borax powder to an ordinary sized kettle of water, in which it should boil. The saving in the quantity of tea will be, at least, one-fifth. To give to black tea the flavor of green tea add a single leaf from the black currant tree.

ARE YOU USING POISONOUS OR ADULTERATED BAKING POWDER?

In view of the immense amount of adulterated baking powders now sold all over the country, we call the attention of consumers to a few facts that may enable them to judge for themselves.

SHORT WEIGHT BAKING POWDERS

are usually adulterated—the heavier true materials being taken out and replaced by some cheap, bulky adulterant to fill the cans, thus giving the consumer bulk instead of weight and purity.

POISONOUS BAKING POWDERS.

These are usually made from Alum, Phosphates, Lime, and other substitutes, instead of pure Grape Cream of Tartar. These powders are usually caked and lumpy, but it requires a chemical analysis to detect their injuriousness; they are usually sold loose or in bulk, and not in cans under label and trade-mark of a responsible manufacturer.

☞ It is not safe to purchase any baking powder loose or in bulk.

CAKED OR LUMPY BAKING POWDERS.

A powder that is found to be caked, may at once be considered defective—they may be composed of substitutes or poisonous adulterants, such as are usually employed in the short weight baking powders—at any rate they are dangerous to use, *and should in all cases be returned to the grocer, and not allowed to go into the kitchen.*

The Royal Baking Powder has been before the public nearly 20 years, and not a single pound of it has ever been known to cake, except through exposure to water in shipment, or some unusual damage not within the power of the manufacturer to prevent.

The Royal Powder is made of absolutely pure materials, and may be relied upon for purity, strength, and wholesomeness. Sold by the best Grocers.

BLANCHARD
Concentrated
BLOOD & NERVE FOOD,
OR
Tonic Extract of Wheat.

A LIQUID FOOD,

Which INVIGORATES and SUSTAINS without stimulating. It contains, in every quart, the vital nutritive elements of a bushel of wheat, the Brain building elements of which are, in this preparation, concentrated so that for every disease where Nervous debility is present (and this is the cause of most chronic diseases) this article of Food is a sure and permanent cure.

Having the Vital Nutritive properties of the Wheat, we call it FOOD, as it really is a FOOD TONIC; it feeds and vitalizes the Nervous tissue, and regulates the digestive organs. By its assimilable properties it is readily absorbed into the circulation, and at once invigorates the impaired faculties.

Every disease associated with an IMPOVERISHED STATE of the BLOOD and general NERVOUS PROSTRATION, will receive from this preparation an immediate and permanent benefit.

All cases of Brain Waste are restored ; Sleeplessness overcome; in fact the whole nervous system re-invigorated and restored.

This Food is adapted to the wants of young or old, male or female: it cures because it is a natural remedy, and has no drug element, being purely and simply a Wheat Tonic.

AGENTS WANTED.

Sold by authorized Agents and Druggists generally.

BLANCHARD FOOD CURE CO.,
27 Union Square, N. Y.

Mrs. LIZZIE S. HUBBARD, Agent.
284 Fulton Street, Brooklyn.

Testimonials of leading physicians of this city furnished on application. Circulars sent free. Lady Physicians in attendance.

Having used the "Blanchard Food" in my family, and finding it all that is represented to be, I take pleasure in recommending it.
MRS. MERWIN, First Directress of the "Home."

WATERS' ORCHESTRION chime ORGANS are the most beautiful in style and perfect in tone ever made. Having the celebrated Concerto stop, which is a fine imitation of the Human Voice, and two and a half Octaves of bells tuned in perfect harmony with the reeds, their effect is magical and electrifying. WATERS' CLARIONA, ORCHESTRAL BELL, CONCERTO, VESPER, CENTENNIAL Chimes, CHAPEL, FAVORITE, SOUVENIR and BOUDOIR ORGANS, in Unique French Cases combine PURITY of VOICING with great volume of tone; suitable for PARLOR or CHURCH.

WATERS' PIANOS, GRAND, SQUARE, and UPRIGHT ARE THE BEST MADE. The Tone, Touch, Workmanship, and Durability Unsurpassed. Warranted for SIX YEARS. PRICES EXTREMELY LOW for cash. Monthly Installments received. Instruments to let until paid for as per contract. A Liberal Discount to Teachers, Ministers, Churches, Schools, Lodges, etc. AGENTS WANTED. Illustrated Catalogues Mailed. Second-hand Pianos and Organs at GREAT BARGAINS. HORACE WATERS & SONS, Manufacturers and Dealers, 40 E. 14th St.

A QUESTION ANSWERED.
It is a question often asked "How is it that HORACE WATERS & SONS have attained the Front Rank while so many other houses are at a stand still?" In answer to this we would say that during our business experience of over 25 years, we have given our customers in every instance the value of their money. Call and see us before purchasing an ORGAN or PIANO. HORACE WATERS & SONS, 40 E. 14th St., W. of Broadway, N.Y.

CONSUMPTION, Weak Lungs, Throat Diseases, General Debility, Dyspepsia or Indigestion, Scrofulous Affections, and all Diseases caused by an Impaired Vigor of the Brain, Loss of Nervous Power and Energy, or Poverty of the Blood, speedily and radically cured, by

Winchester's Hypophosphite of Lime & Soda.

THIS GRAND SPECIFIC,

Established 20 Years,

Has performed most wonderful cures, and accomplished results which no other remedy, preparation or treatment has ever equaled or even approached. TRY IT!

Prices, $1 and $2 per Bottle.

Prepared only by

WINCHESTER & CO., Chemists,

Sold by Druggists.   No. 36 JOHN STREET, NEW YORK.

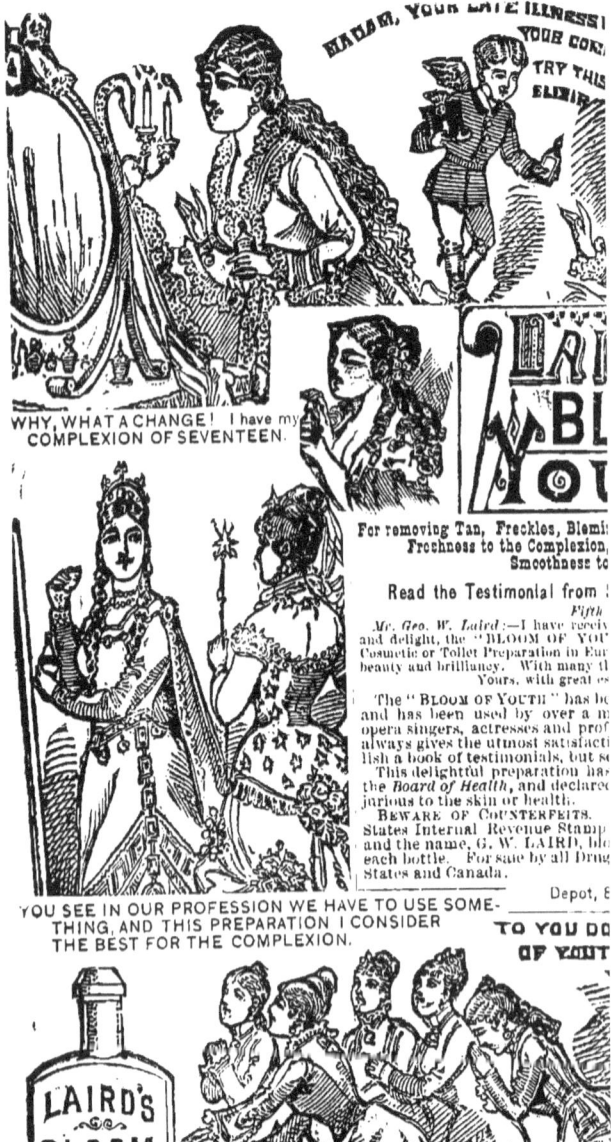

WECHSLER, ABRAHAM & CO.
IMPORTERS AND DEALERS IN
DRY GOODS
297 & 299 Fulton St., and 266 & 268 Washington St.,
BROOKLYN.

S. YOUNG'S POPULAR STORE,
349 Myrtle Avenue, near Adelphi,
Sole Importer of the Celebrated "Carrie" Kid,
PRICE, $1.19.
Manufacturer of Ladies' and Infants' Muslin Outfits and Corsets.
IMMENSE STOCK OF HOSIERY, EMBROIDERIES AND LACES.

We take pleasure in inviting you to an inspection of a *fine line* of the very popular *English* and *Other Styles* of *Wall Papers* and *Interior Decorations*, comprising *Fillings, Dados, Friezes, Borders, Mouldings, etc.* These goods cannot be excelled for *richness* of *design* or *harmony* of *coloring*.

In our *Upholstery Department* will be found a *Complete Assortment* of *Lace Curtains, Furniture Coverings, Window Shades, Pier and Mantle Mirrors, Pole Cornices, Cretonnes, Tassels, Fringes, Gimps*, etc., etc.

W. & H. MUMFORD,
N. B.—Agents for the Long Island Lace Curtain Bleachery. 390 & 392 FULTON ST.

NOTED FOR QUALITY AND CLEANLINESS.

SCHEPP'S
THE ONLY GENUINE COCOANUT,
FOR
Pies, Puddings, Cakes, Tarts, etc.

In purchasing ask for "SCHEPP'S" COCOANUT, and see that the package has a fresh appearance. A trial will prove its merits.

LYMAN A. GILL. PRIOR F. PURDY.

GILL & PURDY,
Carpet Warehouse,
257 FULTON ST.,
Opposite Clinton St., BROOKLYN, N. Y.

STANDARD MAKES OF CARPETINGS.

The tendency among merchants and manufacturers to meet the demand for lower prices has resulted in the offering, by not a few of the carpet dealers, of large lines of carpetings at apparently low prices, which so far as durability is considered, are almost worthless. These goods are sold upon the manufacturer's reputation earned in better times, but who have now reduced the quality rather than be content with small profits. Messrs. GILL & PURDY, Carpet Warehouse, 257 Fulton St., opp. Clinton, late Foster Bros., offer those of manufacturers only who have maintained the standard of their goods.

KNICKERBOCKER
Life Insurance Company,
239 BROADWAY, N. Y.
CHARTERED IN 1853.

JOHN A. NICHOLS, President.

Accumulated Assets, over - - *$6,000,000.00*
Surplus, over - - - *500,000.00*

EVERY DESIRABLE FORM OF POLICY ISSUED.

SAVINGS BANK POLICIES A SPECIALTY.

GEO. F. SNIFFEN, Secretary.   CHAS. M. HIBBARD, Actuary.
E. W. DERBY, M.D., Medical Examiner.   HENRY W. JOHNSON, Counsel.
JOHN F. NICHOLS, Cashier.

GROCERIES.

All goods bearing our name are guaranteed to be of good quality, and dealers are authorized to refund the purchase price in any case where consumers have cause for dissatisfaction. Look for the name,

THURBERS.

ESTABLISHED 1844.

D. K. DUCKER & CO.

Nos. 42 & 44 Fulton Street,

BROOKLYN

CRACKER BAKERY,

Fine Crackers and Biscuits,

EVERY VARIETY FOR FAMILY USE.

Wholesale and Retail Depot, 12 & 44 Fulton St.

Sold by Grocers and dealers universally.

FINE GRADES OF FAMILY FLOUR.

WILLIAM BERRI'S SONS.

(ESTABLISHED 1848.)

CARPETING

526 FULTON STREET,

E. D. BERRI,
WM. BERRI.

BROOKLYN.

FREDERICK  LOESER & CO.
Fulton, Tillary and   Washington Streets,

OUR LEADING MERCHANTS.

Dry Goods, Fancy Goods,

Millinery, Straw Goods,

LADIES' AND CHILDREN'S

FINE BOOTS AND SHOES.

BEST QUALITIES! LOWEST PRICES!

D. H. GILDERSLEEVE & CO.,
MANUFACTURING
STATIONERS,

Blank Receipts,
Drafts, Notes,
Brokers' Pads,
Blank Books,
Bill and Receipt Books,
Letter Books,
etc., etc.
Bill and Legal Cap.

Pens, Pencils, Pen-racks, Ink stands, and all kinds of Ink and Writing Fluids.
Mucilage in all Sizes.
Elastic Bands.
Letter and Note Papers.

BLANK BOOKS
OF ANY PATTERN
Manufactured to Order.

BILL HEADS, NOTE HEADS, AND LETTER HEADS,
CHECK BOOKS, BANK PASS BOOKS, DRAFT BOOKS.

101 CHAMBERS STREET, NEW YORK.

POND'S EXTRACT

The Vegetable Pain Destroyer and Invaluable Family Remedy.
FOR BURNS AND SCALDS IT IS WITHOUT AN EQUAL.
Healing, Comforting. It Cures all Inflammatory Diseases.

CAUTION. Some unscrupulous tradesmen, desirous of making a large profit, are in the habit of selling crude imitations of POND'S EXTRACT, representing them as being made from Witch Hazel, and the same as our Remedy. The appearance and odor being fairly counterfeited they are enabled to do this more readily. Beware of all such impositions. Ask for POND'S EXTRACT. Take no other. Be sure the name

Pond's Extract

is blown in the bottle, and our trade-mark is on surrounding wrapper.

FOR SALE BY ALL DRUGGISTS.

Price, 50 Cents for small, $1.00 for medium and $1.75 for large size.

List of Specialties adapted to Sensitive and peculiar Cases, and largely containing the essential properties of the Extract.

Pond's Extract Toilet Cream is Pond's Extract in a condensed form, combined with other ingredients of rare and absolute purity. Price, $1.00 per bottle.

Pond's Extract Dentifrice, or Tooth Wash.—Delightful as a dentifrice, or combined with three parts water as a mouth wash, will strengthen tender gums and stop all bleeding therefrom. Price, 50c. per bot.

Pond's Extract Lip Salve.—Price, 25c. per box.

Pond's Extract Soap.—Peculiarly freshening to the complexion, and invigorating to the person. Price, per box, 3 cakes, 50c.

Pond's Extract Ointment contains all the healing qualities of Pond's Extract. Price, 50c.

The above Trade-Mark is on the surrounding wrapper of bottle, none genuine without it.

Pond's Extract Catarrh Preparation for seriously sensitive and obstinate cases. It is pleasant, cooling and soothing in its application, and contains in their full strength, all the healing properties of the Extract. Price 75c.

Pond's Extract Plasters affords quick relief from pain, and is very strengthening. Price, 15c.

Pond's Extract Nasal Syringe for use in Catarrh, &c. Price, 25c.

Inhaler, superior in quality. Price, $1.00.

THE POND EXTRACT CO., New York and London.
For use of other diseases, and further directions, consult POND'S EXTRACT BOOK, supplied by any Druggist gratis.

WEDDING STATIONERY,
Invitations, etc,

D. H. GILDERSLEEVE & CO.,
101 CHAMBERS STREET, NEW YORK.

www.ingramcontent.com/pod-product-compliance
Lightning Source LLC
Chambersburg PA
CBHW032149230426
43672CB00011B/2501